孫子兵法

Dedicated to my father, Franklin (1918-1966),
a survivor of the Battan Death March,
and all those who, like him, have fought and died for freedom

Art of War Gift Book Titles

The Mastering Strategy Series

^{Sun Tzu's} The Art of War Plus The Ancient Chinese Revealed
See the original! Each original Chinese character individually translated.

^{Sun Tzu's} The Art of War Plus Its Amazing Secrets
Learn the hidden secrets! The deeper meaning of *bing-fa* explained.

The Warrior Class: 306 Lessons in Strategy
The complete study guide! The most extensive analysis of *The Art of War* ever written.

Career and Business Series

^{Sun Tzu's} The Art of War Plus The Art of Career Building
For everyone! Use Sun Tzu's lessons to advance your career.

^{Sun Tzu's} The Art of War Plus The Art of Sales
For salespeople! Use Sun Tzu's lessons to win sales and keep customers.

^{Sun Tzu's} The Art of War Plus The Art of Management
For managers! Use Sun Tzu's lessons one managing teams more effectively.

^{Sun Tzu's} The Art of War Plus Strategy for Sales Managers
For managers! Use Sun Tzu's lessons to direct salespeople more effectively.

^{Sun Tzu's} The Art of War Plus The Art of Small Business
For business owners! Use Sun Tzu's lessons in building your own business.

^{Sun Tzu's} The Art of War Plus The Art of Marketing
For marketing professionals! Use Sun Tzu's lessons to win marketing warfare.

Life Strategies Series

^{Sun Tzu's} The Art of War Plus The Warrior's Apprentice
A first book of strategy for young adults.

^{Sun Tzu's} The Art of War Plus The Art of Love
For lifelong love! *Bing-fa* applied to finding, winning, and keeping love alive.

^{Sun Tzu's} The Art of War Plus The Art of Parenting Teens
For every parent! Strategy applied to protecting, guiding, and motivating teens.

Current Events Series

^{Sun Tzu's} The Art of War Plus Strategy against Terror
An examination of the War on Terror using Sun Tzu's timeless principles.

Audio and Video

Amazing Secrets of The Art of War: Audio with book
1 1/2 Hours 2 CD set

Amazing Secrets of *The Art of War:* Video with book
1 1/2 Hours VHS

孫子兵法

Sun Tzu's
THE
ART
OF
WAR

Plus
Book Series

Strategy against Terror

Ancient Wisdom for Today's War

孫子兵法

Sun Tzu's
THE
ART
OF
WAR

Plus
Book Series

Strategy against Terror

Ancient Wisdom for Today's War

By Gary Gagliardi

Clearbridge Publishing

Published by
Clearbridge Publishing

FIRST EDITION, 2nd printing

Printed in China.
Interior and cover graphic design by Dana and Jeff Wincapaw.
Original Chinese calligraphy by Tsai Yung, Green Dragon Arts, www.greendragonarts.com.

Publisher's Cataloging-in-Publication Data
Sun-tzu, 6th cent. B.C.
      [Sun-tzu ping fa, English]
      The art of war plus strategy against terror / Sun Tzu; Gary Gagliardi.
      p. 192 cm. 23
      Includes glossary of key Chinese concepts
      ISBN 1-929194-31-5 (hardcover)
      1. Military art and science - Early works to 1800. 2. Competition. I. Gagliardi, Gary 1951— . II.
Title.
U101'.S9513 2003
355'.02 — dc19
                        Library of Congress Catalog Card Number: 2004105755

Clearbridge Publishing's books may be purchased for business, for any promotional use, or for special sales. Please contact:

Clearbridge
Clearbridge Publishing
Art of War Gift Books
PO Box 33772, Seattle, WA 98133
Phone: (206)533-9357 Fax: (206)546-9756
www.ArtOfWarGiftBooks.com

Contents

The Art of War Plus
Strategy Against Terror

Key Dates in Modern Islamic Terror

November 4, 1979: Khomeini takes over US embassy in Iran.
April 18, 1983: US embassy in Beirut bombed, 17 killed.
October 23, 1983: Marine HQ in Beirut bombed, 239 killed.
December 12, 1983: US embassy in Kuwait bombed, 6 killed.
September 20, 1984: US embassy in Beirut bombed, 14 killed.
December 4, 1984: Kuwaiti Airbus hijacked, 2 Americans killed.
June 14, 1985: TWA flight to Rome hijacked, 1 American killed.
October 7, 1985: ship *Achille Lauro* hijacked, 1 American killed.
November 23, 1985: Egyptian Boeing 737 hijacked, 57 killed.
December 27, 1985: attacks on Rome and Vienna airports, 18 killed.
April 2, 1986: TWA flight to Athens bombed, 4 killed.
April 5, 1986: discotheque in West Berlin bombed, 1 killed.
September 5: 1986, Pan Am 747 stormed in Karachi, 21 killed.
September 6: 1986, synagogue in Istanbul attacked, 21 killed.
April 5, 1988: Kuwaiti 747 hijacked to Algeria, 2 killed.
December 21, 1988: Pan Am 747 bombed in Lockerbie, 259 killed.
August 2, 1990–February 27, 1991: Kuwait invaded and America responds.
February 26, 1993: NY World Trade Center bombed, 6 killed.
October 4, 1993: in Mogadishu, Somalia, 17 Marines killed.
December 24, 1994: French Airbus to Paris hijacked, 3 killed.
July 25, 1995: Paris commuter train bombed, 4 killed.
November 13, 1996: bombing in Riyadh, 6 Americans killed.
April 4, 1996: Cairo hotel attacked, 18 Western tourists killed.
June 25, 1996: Khobar Towers truck bombing, 19 Americans killed.
February 23, 1997: Empire State Building shooting, 1 killed.
September 18, 1997: Cairo tourist bus bombed, 10 tourists killed.
November 17, 1997: attack on tourists in Luxor, Egypt, 70 killed.
August 7, 1998: Kenya's and Tanzania's US embassies bombed, 270 killed.
December 28, 1998: tourists kidnapped in Yemen, 4 killed.
October 31, 1999: Egypt Air pilot suicides off NY, 217 killed.
October 12, 2000: USS *Cole* bombed, 17 killed.
December 31, 2000: five bombs explode in Manila, 14 killed.
September 11, 2001: World Trade Center attacked, 2,700 killed.
October 5, 2001: anthrax attacks in D.C., 5 killed.
October 7, 2001–present: America counterattacks in Afghanistan and Iraq.
March 11, 2004: Madrid trains bombed, 190 killed.

Introduction

Strategy and Terror

Sun Tzu developed the most powerful strategic system of all time. In this book, we apply his principles directly to winning the war against terrorism. In this introduction, we present Sun Tzu's key concepts and how they apply to fighting terror.

Sun Tzu wrote succinctly, offering his ideas in a very compact format. Like Euclid's *Geometry*, *The Art of War* offers a set of basic concepts that build one upon the other and have a wide variety of specific applications. In this book, we show Sun Tzu's words on the left-hand pages and apply them specifically to the challenge of defeating terrorism on the facing right-hand pages.

Our instinctual reaction to threat is the "flight or fight" reflex. Sun Tzu taught that both of these natural reactions—running away from challenges or getting into meaningless conflict—lead eventually to disaster. Instead, Sun Tzu taught the strategy of advancing our position into openings created by our opponents. Strong positions make us difficult to attack and, over time, convince others to join us.

Since Sun Tzu's work is about positioning, he organizes the work around the five concepts that define competitive positions. These five factors—philosophy, the ground, the climate, the leader, and methods—provide the framework of his system. In this introduction, we use these five factors to create an overview of using Sun Tzu's strategy against terror.

This analysis begins by seeing war as a battle between philosophies. The War on Terror is a battle of the ideal of freedom against the ideal of moral totalitarianism. Contrary to what we hear in the media, terrorists are not driven by anti-American philosophy. Their philosophy is much older than the existence of the United States.

Sun Tzu admonishes us to learn from the history of war. Fundamentalist battles within the Islamic world are as old as the religion itself. In 657, the Kharijites became Islam's first dogmatic, fanatical sect fighting for power through dogmatism. The pattern of fundamentalist schism has been repeated many times throughout Islamic history. The Wahhabis started as puritanical reformers and rose to conquer Mecca in 1806, only to be later defeated by the Muslim Turks. The Ikhwan, the Wahhabi followers of Ibn Saud, reconquered Mecca in 1924, and Saudi Arabia, the country founded by Ibn Saud, is the main source of today's Wahhabi movement.

These fanatical movements were each resisted and eventually stopped by the mainstream Muslim community itself. From the Kharijites to the Ikhwan, fundamentalist Islamic sects viewed other Muslims as no different from infidels. Ali, the fourth caliph, defeated the Kharijites in 658 at Nahrawan. Similarly, Ibn Saud turned against the Ikhwan at the Battle of Sibilla in 1929.

Like these earlier sects, today's Islamic fanatics want to seize power forcibly on the basis of reforming their less dogmatic fellow Muslims. Only secondarily do they want to convert, conquer, or kill all those who are not Muslims. Fortunately, their numbers are too few to accomplish any of these goals. To succeed they must spread their philosophy and grow their organizations.

America represents a philosophy that is the polar opposite of this religious totalitarianism. We stand for freedom, which terrorists see as the freedom to sin. We stand for democracy, which represents the rule of the non-fundamentalist majority. We also represent the rise of the West and Christianity over Islam during the last six hundred years. America, like Israel, is a useful target for terrorists. However, their historical mission has always been gaining acceptance in the Islamic world. By identifying America as the enemy, terrorists hope to rally and unite their fellow Muslims.

After philosophy, the next key factor we must understand is the ground. In Sun Tzu's system, the ground is what sustains the army and provides its resources. Sun Tzu teaches that wars depend on economics. Unless the ground supports an army, the army cannot fight. The ground is where we fight to win control of key resources. By this standard, what is the battleground for the terrorists? How do they get rewarded for winning control of this ground?

At this point, terrorists aren't fighting for physical ground. Most of the world's billion Muslims live in police states. The terrorists' goal is not to destroy these totalitarian societies but to control them. Though controlling these states is the long-term goal, these physical states are not the current battleground. First, the terrorists must build up their organizations and finances.

To build their organizations, they need recruits and donations. How does killing innocent people generate donations and recruits? Kidnapping and extortion can raise money directly, but terrorists have found that bombing or attacking public buildings and means of transportation works much better. How do these seemingly senseless deaths generate recruits and money? They get news coverage. This free publicity generates financial support and recruits. The murder of innocents is an advertising campaign that makes terrorists seem powerful and spreads their philosophy. Terrorists are fighting a media war. Their chosen battleground is the television screen and the newspaper front page.

This battleground is connected to what Sun Tzu calls "the climate." This is the next key factor in strategic analysis. The climate is the realm of uncontrollable change. It includes not only the weather, but social, cultural, and business changes as well. Climate shifts in the battleground bring opposing philosophies into actual conflict. How has the climate in the media changed to bring terrorism to the fore? Isn't the media just reporting the news?

Until Vietnam, thugs like the terrorists were routinely savaged by the morally indignant—rather than morally neutral—media. Al Qaeda's philosophy of religious superiority is nearly identical to the racial superiority beliefs of the German Nazi party and American Ku Klux Klan. In the 1930s and 1940s, the American press universally condemned the Nazis. In the fifties and sixties, the media was just as consistent in condemning the Klan. Reporters applauded the brave sacrifices made to stop tyranny and oppression. Victories were celebrated. Fascists were portrayed as madmen that no sane person could support. The media had a moral compass. Unfortunately, this climate has changed.

Since Vietnam, the increasingly morally neutral, politically correct media claims that it doesn't take sides, but it reports from a standard script. That script is the story of David versus Goliath. The media casts America in the role of Goliath. It casts whoever opposes America as David. The press of today therefore doesn't condemn terrorists like the press once criticized the Nazis and the Klan. We don't see prime-time specials exposing the cruelty and viciousness of terrorist organizations. The news agency Reuters doesn't even use the word "terrorist" because it makes a moral judgment about those who make a practice of killing innocent people. This is the climate that makes the terrorist advertising program possible.

The media also uses its David-versus-Goliath script to characterize corporations as evil. Imagine if, instead of terrorists, a corporation were publicly murdering people to advertise its product. Would members of the press cooperate in the same way as they have with terrorism? After every murder, would they wait for the corporation's announcement claiming credit? Would the media promote negotiations, tolerance, and understanding of that corporation's needs despite its methods? Of course not.

In the media war, terrorists are refining their message. Al Qaeda's founder, Abdullah Azzam, described his mission simply as "Jihad and the rifle alone: no negotiations, no conferences and no dialogues." Its goal was overthrowing "the godless regimes" in the Middle East, with no mention of America or the Palestinians. By 1998, bin Laden had added the media's David-versus-Goliath script, "the United States is occupying the lands of Islam in the holiest of its territories, Arabia, plundering its riches, overwhelming its rulers, humiliating its people..." Bin Laden further strengthened this message in 2004 by adding the press's favorite evil corporation: "This war makes millions of dollars for big corporations, either weapons manufacturers or those working in the reconstruction [of Iraq], such as Halliburton and its sister companies..." Then, in his video released right before the U.S. presidential election, bin Laden echoed every charge in Michael Moore's propaganda film because it as typifying what the media wanted to hear.

By playing to the media's prejudices, terrorists have discovered that it can get virtually unlimited free non-judgmental advertising as long as it keeps up its killing and hostage-taking. Unfortunately, Sun Tzu teaches us that we cannot control a battleground's climate, especially the climate in the media. The climate changes naturally over time. We can, however, change the battleground. This is the role of leaders and methods, the last two key factors in strategy.

Sun Tzu teaches that methods must conform to the organization's core philosophy. These methods determine the shape of the organization. Terrorists are defined by their methods. They intentionally threaten innocent people to blackmail others into cooperation. Terrorists leverage the compassion of their enemies against them. While America may unavoidably kill civilians in going after terrorists, our actions are not terrorism because it is not our goal to kill innocents. On the other hand, leaders like Saddam Hussein, Kim Jong Il, or the late Yassar Arafat do satisfy this definition of terrorism because they intentionally their own nations as hostage. Sun Tzu's framework can be used to analyze the weaknesses and strengths of terrorists' methods and their organizations.

Terrorist leaders such as bin Laden changed the rules when they discovered that by directing their threats and blackmail against non-Muslims—Jews, Americans, and Europeans—they could get broader support for fundamentalism from within the Muslim world. Sun Tzu teaches us that we must fight on our opponent's home ground rather than our own. By attacking innocent Jews and Westerners, terrorists are following this dictate.

An Al Qaeda training manual recently discovered in Manchester, England, explains the terrorists' organization and its methods in detail. The focus is primarily on growing the organization, recruiting new members, testing them, training them, organizing them, and so on. When the manual suggests acts of terror, it gives public places a higher priority than political or economic institutions. Why? They are less secure and generate better news coverage.

From the manual, we learn to see Al Qaeda as a secret brotherhood providing a sense of belonging for its members. Most of its methods—secret signs, setting up meetings, raising and handling donations—would be familiar to the Masons, Lions, and Rotary.

Why is a secret brotherhood so appealing to young Muslims? Most Muslims live in police states. While most people in the world put their efforts into economic competition, these states are often described as "kleptocracies" that extort tribute for any economic activity. The Heritage Foundation lists virtually every Muslim state in the "mostly unfree" or "repressed" categories in its *Index of Economic Freedom*. Al Qaeda appeals to frustrated young people with no productive outlet for their aspirations.

Al Qaeda's training manual teaches how to attract members

through coercion, greed, the offer of adventure and amusement, and fear. Al Qaeda doesn't solicit the most religious members of society. It rates smugglers as the best potential recruits.

There are over a billion Muslims. If only one Muslim out of ten thousand (one thousandth of 1 percent) joins Al Qaeda, that makes one hundred thousand members. This is the base (*al qaeda* means "base") of a substantial pyramid. Out of this hundred thousand, only a few hundred become "commanders" who collect money, organize meetings, solicit new members, and so on. Like any pyramid scheme, local organizations channel funds up to the parent organization.

Lower in the pyramid, local Al Qaeda cells have limited abilities, but there are many of them. On average, they are relatively harmless no matter how bloody their intentions. Few cells get their hands on explosives or have the skill to plan a local bombing. A truly rare cell can plan an attack like the Madrid bombing. It is their numbers that make these cells dangerous. Out of this large network, a few talented individuals can rise and get the resources necessary to wreak havoc.

How can we create a workable method to fight this large network of independent cells? Sun Tzu's strategy doesn't suggest just one method to counter our enemies but a host of them. In adapting Sun Tzu's concepts to the War on Terror, we cover a wide variety of approaches through the course of this book.

To destroy Al Qaeda and similar terror organizations, we must undermine the pyramid on which it is based. Of course, we must never give into the blackmail and hostage-taking that is the basis of terrorism. Since Al Qaeda creates support through the media, we must address the message the potential recruits and donors hear through the press. By killing terrorists, we can fill the news media with stories of their defeat. As bin Laden himself said, "When people see a strong horse and a weak horse, by nature, they will like the strong horse." When it is clear that the terrorists' strategy has brought nothing but more defeat to the Islamic world, Muslims will rethink investing sons and dollars in the effort.

Moving the physical battleground to the Middle East forces mainstream Muslims to confront the heritage of terror. After Afghanistan and Iraq, terrorists returned to attacking their fellow Muslims in Turkey, Saudi Arabia, Pakistan, and even Uzbekistan. These states are increasing their activities against terror. This exposes much of Al Qaeda's hidden structure. As war opponents predicted, we stirred up an anthill by moving into Iraq, but it is the ants and their hidden organizations that are suffering. They are less dangerous out in the open than they are building and burrowing underground. Even when terrorists move into Iraq to fight Americans, they are helping us. Unlike the media battle, fighting our army in the field is extremely costly. It pressures their limited financial resources and eliminates their most dedicated members.

As Sun Tzu says, when we go to war, we cannot know all the dangers of using arms, but we cannot know all the benefits either. Though the press continually reemphasizes how we didn't find Saddam's chemical or biological weapons, the biggest benefit of the war in Iraq was that it uncovered a secret plot to move nuclear weapons into the area from North Korea through Pakistan. This plot to spread nuclear weapons throughout the region was the single greatest danger to human life on earth. Though they get scant attention in the press, the nuclear weapons that we have uncovered in Libya and Iran are as dangerous to our safety as the weapons of mass destruction (WMDs) that have gone missing.

Longer term, we must provide positive alternatives for the people of Islam. When people's political and economic options are limited, they are tempted by terrorism as a "career path." As long as the Muslim world lives under tyranny, poisonous secret organizations will continue to exist and command a sympathetic following.

In Afghanistan and Iraq, we have potentially carved out some free space within a world of tyranny. These areas can provide Muslims with a beacon of freedom. It may take years to realize this dream, but the examples of Iraq and Afghanistan are already having an impact on Libya, Syria, Iran, and other Islamic nations.

As America has been destined to fight against the tyrannies of monarchy, fascism, and communism, we must commit ourselves to a media war, a message war, against Islamic tyranny. This is a religious war—not of Christianity against Islam, but of those who support God's gift of freedom against those who want to compel religious belief to justify their own rise to power.

The Islamic world has always been divided, not only by religious differences but by ancient clan and tribal conflicts. These groups have continually fought against one another for dominance. We must fight for the idea that constitutional democracy, in which the rights of minorities are protected, is the Creator's ultimate political solution for the need for unity among the *umma*, the Islamic brotherhood.

Muslims must see that freedom, opportunity, democracy, *and* Islam are all gifts from God. During the Dark Ages in Europe, Muslims were the most tolerant, educated, and civilized people in the world. Jews moved to Muslim countries to *escape* persecution. Promoting the values of the Islamic golden age would be a powerful alternative to the failed policies of Al Qaeda, Hezbollah, Hamas, Islamic Jihad, and the other divisive forces of terrorism.

Over time, Sun Tzu says, the climate changes. Eventually, Islamic terrorism will seem as meaningless as fascism or devil worship. Until then, we must use all our strategic skills to stem the tide of terror. The purpose of this book is to spread an understanding of those skills.

✦ ✦ ✦

Chapter 1

Analysis: Freedom versus Terror

Sun Tzu begins his work by forcing us to analyze our situation in comparison to that of our opponents. With a deeper understanding of our relative strengths and weaknesses, we start developing the framework for making the right decisions. Most importantly, the framework focuses on the unique aspects of the conflict.

Every conflict is unique. Without analysis, we naturally tend to fight the current war using the techniques that were successful in the last war. In the battle against terror, our natural tendency is to frame religious fanaticism in the same terms in which we framed the battle against communism. This problem is accentuated by the media, which plays a key role in this battle. While our government largely recognizes how different this battle is from the Cold War, members of the media are still reacting to Vietnam.

In the chapter's first section, Sun Tzu describes the major components that define our opposing positions; the interrelationships between these components are key to establishing a successful position against terrorism.

The chapter's final major topic is deception or illusion, which plays a central role in all wars but is especially important in the War on Terror. By providing a false vision of their organizations, Al Qaeda and other terrorist organizations are putting us in the position of fighting with phantoms. As we will see, we must combat their illusions with deceptions of our own.

Analysis

SUN TZU SAID:

This is war. 1
It is the most important skill in the nation.
It is the basis of life and death.
It is the philosophy of survival or destruction.
You must know it well.

[6]Your skill comes from five factors.
Study these factors when you plan war.
You must insist on knowing your situation.

1.	Discuss philosophy.
2.	Discuss the climate.
3.	Discuss the ground.
4.	Discuss leadership.
5.	Discuss military methods.

[14]It starts with your military philosophy.
Command your people in a way that gives them a higher
shared purpose.
You can lead them to death.
You can lead them to life.
They must never fear danger or dishonesty.

Freedom versus Terror

1 To win the War on Terror, we cannot fool ourselves. This is a battle to the death. Either the terrorists will succeed in destroying our modern world or we will destroy them. We may see ourselves as richer and more powerful than they are, but over the length of this battle, it is only our strategy skills that matter.

Our strategic position and that of the terrorists are defined by five factors. These factors play into every part of the battle. Without understanding each of these factors, we cannot understand our situation. We must understand both our philosophy and that of the terrorists. We must understand how the trends of the time affect our contest. We must understand the true battleground in this war. We must know the relative strengths of our form of leadership and the methods that we employ in this battle.

Like the Cold War, the War on Terror is a battle of philosophies. We see ourselves as fighting for the rule of law and freedom against religious fanaticism and intolerance. The terrorists frame this as a battle between corrupt materialism and religious and moral standards. We and the terrorists agree that the United States represents the force of life while they represent the power of death.

[19]Next, you have the climate.
It can be sunny or overcast.
It can be hot or cold.
It includes the timing of the seasons.

[23]Next is the terrain.
It can be distant or near.
It can be difficult or easy.
It can be open or narrow.
It also determines your life or death.

[28]Next is the commander.
He must be smart, trustworthy, caring, brave, and strict.

[30]Finally, you have your military methods.
They shape your organization.
They come from your management philosophy.
You must master their use.

[34]All five of these factors are critical.
As a commander, you must pay attention to them.
Understanding them brings victory.
Ignoring them means defeat.

Climate is not just the physical weather but the social climate, especially in the media, and the changes in attitude that affect our struggle against terror. This climate changes constantly over time but some of its shifts are cyclic and predictable.

What battleground have the terrorists chosen? The ground supports the organization, generating its resources and income. Where are terrorists fighting to win resources? The answer is in the world press. The physical attacks win attention in the press and generate the recruits and donations that keep terrorism alive.

To win, our leaders must be more clever, dedicated, sensitive, courageous, and resolved than the terrorist leaders.

Our methods rely on promoting the freedom of Western civilization. The terrorists use hostage-taking and blackmail, leveraging the morally neutral media to advertise their semiautonomous network. We must master new methods to counter them.

To be successful against terror, we must clarify our philosophy, leverage shifts in climate, understand both the physical and media battleground, pick good leaders, and use the methods that best counter the terrorists. Weakness in any of these areas will be fatal.

You must learn through planning. 2
You must question the situation.

³You must ask:
Which government has the right philosophy?
Which commander has the skill?
Which season and place has the advantage?
Which method of command works?
Which group of forces has the strength?
Which officers and men have the training?
Which rewards and punishments make sense?
This tells when you will win and when you will lose.
Some commanders perform this analysis.
If you use these commanders, you will win.
Keep them.
Some commanders ignore this analysis.
If you use these commanders, you will lose.
Get rid of them.

Plan an advantage by listening. 3
Adjust to the situation.
Get assistance from the outside.
Influence events.
Then planning can find opportunities and give you control.

2 To create a successful strategy against terror, we must question our basic assumptions about terrorists and their position.

> We must ask ourselves some serious questions.
> Is our philosophy more appealing than the terrorists' philosophy?
> Are we picking better leaders to fight in a war than they are?
> What battleground should we fight the terrorists on?
> How well does our hierarchy work against their loose network?
> Are we more united and focused than the terrorists are?
> Are our people better prepared to fight than the terrorists are?
> What incentives encourage terrorism? What actions deter it?
> We must pick our leaders based upon how well they understand strategy and how dedicated they are to objective analysis and asking honest questions. If we pick leaders who can see the world objectively without being tainted by their politics, we will succeed against terror. If we pick leaders whose politics dictate what they think and do, we will lose. We have to actively weed out politicians who cannot objectively understand the battle we are in.

3 Good leaders must be judged by their skill at listening rather than their ability to talk. Good leaders are flexible, changing their tactics—but not their beliefs—based on the situation. They embrace outsider viewpoints. They can shape events. Only these types of leaders can find the opportunity to succeed in this war.

Warfare is one thing. 4
It is a philosophy of deception.

³When you are ready, you try to appear incapacitated.
When active, you pretend inactivity.
When you are close to the enemy, you appear distant.
When far away, you pretend you are near.

⁷You can have an advantage and still entice an opponent.
You can be disorganized and still be decisive.
You can be ready and still be preparing.
You can be strong and still avoid battle.
You can be angry and still stop yourself.
You can humble yourself and still be confident.
You can be relaxed and still be working.
You can be close to an ally and still part ways.
You can attack a place without planning to do so.
You can leave a place without giving away your plan.

¹⁷You will find a place where you can win.
You cannot first signal your intentions.

4 Like all wars, the outcome of the War on Terror depends on which side is able to control the perceptions of its opponents.

The terrorists leverage the media to make themselves appear larger and more powerful than they are. They will try to appear inactive when they are really planning an attack. Their chatter will focus on overseas when they are aiming at America.

Though the media will point to America's weaknesses, we are stronger than the terrorists. The media emphasizes our divisions, but our leaders can still act decisively. No matter how superior we are, we can still improve. We are strong because we do not have to fight every battle. When we are insulted, we do not have to respond. Our leaders can humble themselves on the news, and we can still be confident of success. We can afford to be patient because we are successful. We are truly free to attack terrorists when we want, no matter what the media says about us. Our leaders do not have to defend their actions or let the media know what they are planning.

We must find opportunities to leverage the media to undermine the terrorists' ability to predict our behavior.

Manage to avoid battle until your organization can count 5
on certain victory.
You must calculate many advantages.
Before you go to battle, your organization's analysis can indi-
cate that you may not win.
You can count few advantages.
Many advantages add up to victory.
Few advantages add up to defeat.
How can you know your advantages without analyzing them?
We can see where we are by means of our observations.
We can foresee our victory or defeat by planning.

5 We must fight only battles in which we can succeed and publicize our successes. The terrorists and some of the media are always predicting our failure. Every time we are successful, we discredit them publicly and come closer to winning the War on Terror. We must avoid fighting ambiguous battles in which our success is unclear. Afghanistan and Iraq were clear victories. They were not perfect victories, but there are no perfect victories. The terrorists can stir up trouble, but we can still control the ground. We must pursue only opportunities that leverage our strengths. We must objectively analyze our opportunities. We must only undertake actions when we know our goals and know that we can accomplish them.

♦ ♦ ♦

Chapter 2

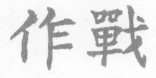

Going to War: The Economics of Terror

Sun Tzu teaches that all war requires economic support. Before the terrorists can go to war, they need money. They need donations, supporting states, and crime to support them. When they take action, the cost of their action must pay for itself in some tangible way. Only when the terrorists no longer have the financial resources to continue their fight will this war grind to a halt. We must understand the financial infrastructure of the terrorist organizations in order to defeat them.

Guns, ammunition, bombs, and the other tools of terror cost money. Weapons of mass destruction are terrifically expensive. As Sun Tzu teaches, good information can often replace weapons. The 9/11 hijackers used only box knives, but the planning and logistics of that attack probably made it Al Qaeda's most costly project.

Where do terrorists get their funds? How are those funds raised? How are they moved throughout the organization? The answers to these questions point up the financial weaknesses and strengths of the terrorist movement. Unless the terrorists get that money, they cannot continue their fight, no matter how dedicated their people.

Though America is the wealthiest nation in the world, we cannot spend an infinite amount of money fighting terror. Sun Tzu teaches us to minimize the cost of war. The economics of war always depend on the will of the people. Who will give up first, the American taxpayer or the terrorist contributor?

Going to War

SUN TZU SAID:

Everything depends on your use of military philosophy. 1
Moving the army requires thousands of vehicles.
These vehicles must be loaded thousands of times.
The army must carry a huge supply of arms.
You need ten thousand acres of grain.
This results in internal and external shortages.
Any army consumes resources like an invader.
It uses up glue and paint for wood.
It requires armor for its vehicles.
People complain about the waste of a vast amount of metal.
It will set you back when you attempt to raise tens of thou-
sands of troops.

12Using a huge army makes war very expensive to win.
Long delays create a dull army and sharp defeats.
Attacking enemy cities drains your forces.
Long violent campaigns that exhaust the nation's resources
are wrong.

The Economics of Terror

1 Terrorist organizations must depend on their Islamic roots
for funding. It takes money to move people and supplies around
the world. These organizations must pay for their weapons and
ammunition. Though many terrorists are volunteers, they must be
fed, housed, clothed, and armed. There is a limit to what terrorists
can afford to do because there is a limit to what their supporters can
and will give. The longer the battle goes on, the more money the
terrorists consume. The more they consume without making real
progress toward Islamic hegemony, the more their supporters will
complain about the costs. These supporters may be dedicated to the
Islamic cause, but they don't want their money to be wasted. The
larger these organizations grow, the more money they consume.

Al Qaeda is a large secret society spread throughout the Muslim
world. Most of its members are in local cells, but they do little more
than participate in local meetings and raise money. Most of these
local organizations are incapable of attacking any defended target.
They will not impoverish themselves to support Al Qaeda.

[16]Manage a dull army.
You will suffer sharp defeats.
You will drain your forces.
Your money will be used up.
Your rivals will multiply as your army collapses and they will
begin against you.
It doesn't matter how smart you are.
You cannot get ahead by taking losses!

[23]You hear of people going to war too quickly.
Still, you won't see a skilled war that lasts a long time.

[25]You can fight a war for a long time or you can make your
nation strong.
You can't do both.

Make no assumptions about all the dangers in using **2**
military force.
Then you won't make assumptions about the benefits of
using arms either.

[3]You want to make good use of war.
Do not raise troops repeatedly.
Do not carry too many supplies.
Choose to be useful to your nation.
Feed off the enemy.
Make your army carry only the provisions it needs.

The base of support required by Al Qaeda is its weak point. Local organizations can be infiltrated. Local cells can be discouraged by pressuring them. If we can isolate Al Qaeda from its base, its resources will be rapidly depleted. As we have seen in Pakistan, Saudi Arabia, and Turkey, the more pressure terrorists are under, the more their opponents within the Islamic world turn against them. Bin Laden and Al Zawahiri may be geniuses, but they cannot survive once their organization is branded as a loser.

Al Qaeda miscalculated in attacking America directly and starting an intense war because the terrorists cannot afford long battles.

We in America also cannot afford to fight an endless war like we had in Vietnam. We must put decisive pressure on Al Qaeda to destroy its resources if we want our country to remain united.

2 Al Qaeda made a mistake. Its leaders correctly assumed that the 9/11 attacks would galvanize their support among Muslims, but they did not realize that it would also galvanize America's opposition against them. Our financial resources vastly outweigh theirs.

Al Qaeda must make its few successful attacks count. There is a limit to how many people will join the organization. There are limits to the amount people will donate. To support their organization, their leaders must advertise successes in our media to leverage our resources against us. However, by threatening their supporters, we can make it increasingly difficult for them to get resources.

The nation impoverishes itself shipping to troops that 3
are far away.
Distant transportation is costly for hundreds of families.
Buying goods with the army nearby is also expensive.
High prices also exhaust wealth.
If you exhaust your wealth, you then quickly hollow out your
military.
Military forces consume a nation's wealth entirely.
War leaves households in the former heart of the nation
with nothing.

[8]War destroys hundreds of families.
Out of every ten families, war leaves only seven.
War empties the government's storehouses.
Broken armies will get rid of their horses.
They will throw down their armor, helmets, and arrows.
They will lose their swords and shields.
They will leave their wagons without oxen.
War will consume 60 percent of everything you have.

Because of this, it is the intelligent commander's duty to 4
feed off the enemy.

[2]Use a cup of the enemy's food.
It is worth twenty of your own.
Win a bushel of the enemy's feed.
It is worth twenty of your own.

3 The one advantage that Al Qaeda has is that it operates locally in the Middle East while we have to support troops that are far away. Fighting so far away is costly to the American taxpayer. Having our armies stationed in the Middle East also changes the economies in that area. Our presence both brings money into the local economy and raises local prices. Some local people benefit, but many suffer. The economic danger is always greater at home. Within America, many domestic opponents of the War on Terror believe that the money spent on the military would be much better spent on social problems closer to home.

What most war opponents fail to realize is that the costs of losing a war are always greater than the costs of winning a war. A successful biological, chemical, or nuclear attack in America could cost hundreds of thousands of lives and wreak havoc on our economy. The blow to our economy would impoverish the government. Even without a devastating terrorist attack, if we pulled all our resources out of the War on Terror today, the progress we have invested in would be wasted. We couldn't convert those resources to another use.

4 To be successful in the War on Terror, we must not only take away the terrorists' resources but use those resources against them.

Since 9/11, we have frozen or appropriated over two hundred million dollars of terrorist funds. We should invest this money in the war against terror. We should work to get laws passed around the world that allow the seizure of terrorists' property like that of drug dealers.

[6]You can kill the enemy and frustrate him as well.
Take the enemy's strength from him by stealing away his
money.

[8]Fight for the enemy's supply wagons.
Capture his supplies by using overwhelming force.
Reward the first who capture them.
Then change their banners and flags.
Mix them in with your own wagons to increase your supply
line.
Keep your soldiers strong by providing for them.
This is what it means to beat the enemy while you grow
more powerful.

Make victory in war pay for itself. 5
Avoid expensive, long campaigns.
The military commander's knowledge is the key.
It determines if the civilian officials can govern.
It determines if the nation's households are peaceful or a
danger to the state.

As an incentive, seized funds and property should go to the law enforcement agencies that make the seizure. We want every local agency to have a financial incentive to infiltrate local terrorist cells.

These incentives would be popular with police forces in the Middle East. Some rich Muslims think of terrorist causes as legitimate charities. This would change dramatically if they saw that they were putting their property at risk by supporting terror. Their entire fortunes could be transferred to local law enforcement agencies. This would give local police a strong incentive to fight terror. Instead of going to arm terrorists, the supporters' resources would then go to those who are fighting terrorism. This would weaken the local network of terror and strengthen local law enforcement.

5 We must gain economic power by fighting terrorists. We must win the war quickly to minimize our costs. We must elect wartime leaders who understand these economics. Only a strong economy will allow our leaders to remain in control. We must manage the war well economically so that taxpayers support the effort rather than blaming the government for terror.

♦ ♦ ♦

Chapter 3

Planning an Attack: Uniting against Terror

Sun Tzu defines an attack as moving into enemy territory. Before we move against any enemy, we have to be assured that we are united both as a nation and as a fighting force. Unity and focus are required at every level of our nation if we are going to be successful in the War on Terror. The goal of unity and focus is not to win the conflict but to succeed while minimizing conflict.

We see how that lack of unity creates unnecessary conflict in the battle for Iraq. Saddam's confidence that Europe would prevent America from attacking encouraged his resistance. He knew that many Europeans, as well as the corrupt bureaucrats of the UN, had a financial incentive to keep him in power. If Europe had stood with America, Saddam would have left the country without a fight.

Sun Tzu lists the basic forms of attack in descending order of importance, from surprise attacks to sieges. He then discusses the tactics of any asymmetrical confrontation when forces of different sizes find themselves in conflict with one another. All these lessons apply directly to the War on Terror.

Sun Tzu also warns that politicians cannot run the army to satisfy a political timetable. After the American experience in Vietnam, we should understand the importance of this warning. Politicizing a war undermines the unity and focus of the nation. As Sun Tzu teaches, our enemies cannot defeat us unless we create the opportunity for them. This is especially true of a war fought in the media.

Planning an Attack

SUN TZU SAID:

Everyone relies on the arts of war. 1
A united nation is strong.
A divided nation is weak.
A united army is strong.
A divided army is weak.
A united force is strong.
A divided force is weak.
United men are strong.
Divided men are weak.
A united unit is strong.
A divided unit is weak.

[12]Unity works because it enables you to win every battle you
fight.
Still, this is the foolish goal of a weak leader.
Avoid battle and make the enemy's men surrender.
This is the right goal for a superior leader.

The best way to make war is to ruin the enemy's plans. 2
The next best is to disrupt alliances.
The next best is to attack the opposing army.
The worst is to attack the enemy's cities.

Uniting against Terror

1 In classical strategy, it is our philosophy (*tao*) that brings people together. If we are united as a nation, we will win the War on Terror. We can only lose if we are divided among ourselves. Our political divisions aside, we are all Americans. Instead of emphasizing the differences among us, we should find common ground in our shared philosophy of democracy and freedom. We have two major parties, but we must support our leaders, even when they belong to the opposition party. We may or may not approve of every military action, but we must always support our men-at-arms. We must turn our backs on those who want to tear our country apart for political reasons. This is what our opponents are counting on.

Our unity will allow us to win our daily battles in the War on Terror, but that is not the central reason why unity is important. If we are united, our opponents will realize that they cannot prevail against us. This will discourage people from joining or contributing to terrorist organizations. People abandon hopeless causes.

2 The best way to move against terrorists is to attack them before they attack us. The next best is to divide terrorists from their supporters. The next best is to hunt down their fighters. The worst is to directly attack their Muslim and media supporters.

⁵This is what happens when you attack a city.
You can attempt it, but you can't finish it.
First you must make siege engines.
You need the right equipment and machinery.
It takes three months and still you cannot win.
Then you try to encircle the area.
You use three more months without making progress.
Your command still doesn't succeed and this angers you.
You then try to swarm the city.
This kills a third of your officers and men.
You are still unable to draw the enemy out of the city.
This attack is a disaster.

Make good use of war. 3
Make the enemy's troops surrender.
You can do this fighting only minor battles.
You can draw their men out of their cities.
You can do it with small attacks.
You can destroy the men of a nation.
You must keep your campaign short.

⁸You must use total war, fighting with everything you have.
Never stop fighting when at war.
You can gain complete advantage.
To do this, you must plan your strategy of attack.

Strategically, a city is a fortified ground position. What are the terrorists' strongholds? They don't have any physical strongholds that can stop our military, but they have established strong psychological positions that cannot be attacked directly. In the media, their position is fortified by anti-American attitudes that grew out of Vietnam. We cannot change those attitudes by attacking them directly. The same is true of attacking the cultural position of the terrorists within the Islamic world. Muslims are looking for champions. They have a cultural prohibition against criticizing fellow Muslims to nonbelievers. Over time, we can win almost all Muslims over to our side in the War on Terror, but not by attacking their Islamic history and traditions.

3 In the long run, we will win this war only one way. We must convince the terrorists that they cannot win. We can do this with quick wars against states that support terror. These wars draw the terrorists' fighters out of hiding and force terrorists to turn on their fellow Muslims. In response, the Muslim community will fight the small, daily battles that will destroy terrorism. We must use our military campaigns for quick strikes instead of long campaigns.

When we are engaged in a specific campaign, like Afghanistan or Iraq, we must use all our resources to win. We must see it through. We can build strong, unassailable positions. We do this strategically by using our advantage of size correctly.

[12]The rules for making war are:
If you outnumber enemy forces ten to one, surround them.
If you outnumber them five to one, attack them.
If you outnumber them two to one, divide them.
If you are equal, then find an advantageous battle.
If you are fewer, defend against them.
If you are much weaker, evade them.

[19]Small forces are not powerful.
However, large forces cannot catch them.

You must master command. 4
The nation must support you.

[3]Supporting the military makes the nation powerful.
Not supporting the military makes the nation weak.

[5]The army's position is made more difficult by politicians in
three different ways.
Ignorant of the whole army's inability to advance, they order
an advance.
Ignorant of the whole army's inability to withdraw, they
order a withdrawal.
We call this tying up the army.
Politicians don't understand the army's business.
Still, they think they can run an army.
This confuses the army's officers.

This is the reality of an asymmetrical war. We must build alliances that isolate the terrorists. Where Muslim states openly support terrorism, we must attack those states. Where the Muslims populace supports terrorism, we must create division. In the media, where America is equated with terrorism, we must pick our battles. Even if the whole world is against us, we must defend ourselves. The terrorists are weaker than we are and must avoid our power.

Our size is both our strength and our weakness. As long as terrorists can hit and run, we will not catch them.

4 We must be able to use our military to defend ourselves. Unlike Vietnam, the nation must support us in the War on Terror.

America needs to support its military to remain strong. Since Vietnam, many vocal Americans have opposed a strong US military.

The source of this attitude is political. Vietnam was a political battlefield as much as it was a physical one. Ignorant of how we could succeed in Vietnam, the politicians sent our military in without a clear idea of how we wanted to advance our position. Politicians limited the military's ability to invade North Vietnam and finally negotiated a treaty that forced our withdrawal. Political considerations tied up our military in a war we could not win. Despite not understanding military strategy, as we saw in Vietnam, politicians think they can control any situation with military force alone. This confuses the military's mission.

¹²Politicians don't know the army's chain of command.
They give the army too much freedom.
This will create distrust among the army's officers.

¹⁵The entire army becomes confused and distrusting.
This invites invasion by many different rivals.
We say correctly that disorder in an army kills victory.

You must know five things to win: 5
Victory comes from knowing when to attack and when to
avoid battle.
Victory comes from correctly using both large and small
forces.
Victory comes from everyone sharing the same goals.
Victory comes from finding opportunities in problems.
Victory comes from having a capable commander and the
government leaving him alone.
You must know these five things.
You then know the theory of victory.

We say: 6
"Know yourself and know your enemy.
You will be safe in every battle.
You may know yourself but not know the enemy.
You will then lose one battle for every one you win.
You may not know yourself or the enemy.
You will then lose every battle."

✦ ✦ ✦

Civilians cannot second-guess military decisions. As we saw in Abu Ghraib, soldiers with too much freedom commit crimes. Still, we cannot let this turn into distrust of our military itself.

If we do not trust our military, our military will be less effective. This will encourage terrorists to act more boldly against us. As we saw in Vietnam, attacking our military leads to certain defeat.

5 To win the War on Terror, we must accomplish five things. First, we must know when we can move against the terrorists and their supporters and when it is better to wait. Next, we must deal with both the small number of active terrorists and the large network that supports them. Third, we must all embrace the idea that democracy and liberty are worth fighting for. Fourth, we must expect problems to arise, realizing that every problem creates a new opportunity. Finally, we must pick the best possible wartime leaders and not allow our political divisions to undermine them. These are not difficult things to do, but all Americans have to understand how important they are to our safety and success.

6 Success in fighting terror depends upon knowledge. The Muslim people must know that America supports their freedom and that the terrorists stand for oppression. If Muslims understand this, we will win every battle. If Muslims want freedom but don't understand that the terrorists want oppression, half our battles will be lost. If Muslims do not believe that America wants their freedom and the terrorists want to enslave them, then we will lose every battle.

Chapter 4

Positioning: In Position to Attack Terror

Strategic philosophy requires that we continually advance our position. The only time we defend is when we cannot find an opportunity to advance. Sun Tzu teaches that positions are dynamic. They are either moving forward or falling back, and falling back is disastrous. The Maginot Line, built by the French to defend themselves from the Germans after World War I, should have proven once and for all that static defensive strategies never work. The only real long-term defense is the credible threat of offensive action.

This philosophy assumes that all retreats are disasters and invitation to more opposition. Failing to defend our established positions encourages our opponents. Our early retreats in Lebanon (1983) and Somalia (1993) convinced the terrorists that we would not defend our positions. In Al Qaeda's 1996 "Declaration of War against the Americans," bin Laden targeted these retreats specifically. Addressing the United States on Lebanon and Somalia, he said, "You have been disgraced by Allah and you withdrew. The extent of your impotence and weaknesses became very clear."

Our enemies are constantly looking for signs of weakness. Our weaknesses provide them with opportunities to advance. In any confrontation, there are only two possible outcomes. Either the terrorists will advance their position or we will advance ours. In the words of the Al Qaeda founder, Abdullah Azzam, "Jihad and the rifle alone: no negotiations, no conferences and no dialogues."

Positioning

SUN TZU SAID:

Learn from the history of successful battles. 1
First, you should control the situation, not try to win.
If you adjust to the enemy, you will find a way to win.
The opportunity to win does not come from yourself.
The opportunity to win comes from your enemy.

6You must pick good battles.
You can control them until you can win.
You cannot win them until the enemy enables your victory.

9We say:
You see the opportunity for victory; you don't create it.

In Position to Attack Terror

1 Before we can act against terrorists, we must first identify their weaknesses. When we explore our opponents' weaknesses, we discover our opportunity to destroy them. As we probe for their weaknesses, we have to defend our current position. This means not showing any weaknesses that invite terrorist attack.

Afghanistan and Iraq were good battles. They advanced our position, taking away the terrorists' sanctuaries and displaying our resolve. We must now look for new opportunities to advance.

We cannot create those opportunities. We must recognize the opportunities that the terrorists and their supporters create for us.

You are sometimes unable to win. 2
You must then defend.
You will eventually be able to win.
You must then attack.
Defend when you have insufficient strength.
Attack when you have a surplus of strength.

7You must defend yourself well.
Save your forces and dig in.
You must attack well.
Move your forces when you have a clear advantage.

11You must always protect yourself until you can completely
triumph.

Some may see how to win. 3
However, they cannot position their forces where they must.
This demonstrates limited ability.

4Some can struggle to a victory and the whole world may
praise their winning.
This also demonstrates a limited ability.

6Win as easily as picking up a fallen hair.
Don't use all of your forces.
See the time to move.
Don't try to find something clever.
Hear the clap of thunder.
Don't try to hear something subtle.

2 Iran and Syria are the two major states offering sanctuary for the terrorists today. However, those states haven't yet given us any cause to move against them. Until they do, we must maintain our positions in Iraq and Afghanistan. Eventually, the states will either reform or create a clear provocation for us to move against them. We must consolidate our current position until they do.

We must commit ourselves to reforming the Middle East. Freedom and prosperity in Iraq and Afghanistan will pressure Iran, Syria, and others to change. Eventually, we will get an opportunity to undermine the oppressive governments in the region.

We must protect ourselves at home and overseas so we can survive long enough for the opportunity for change to present itself.

3 It is easy to see that changing governments in Syria and Iran will advance our position against terror. Our leaders demonstrate their limitations if they fail to find a way to move forward.

The world loves an underdog who wins after overcoming great odds, but fighting those types of battles will not make us successful against terror. Good strategy requires leveraging our opportunities.

Strategy dictates that we seek out situations in which the odds are heavily in our favor. We should never pick battles that require all of our forces at once. Instead, we should provide the key forms of support at key times. We don't need big plans and complex ideas. There are insurgents in Iran and Syria. We should support them. When our opponents actively provoke us, we should go after them.

[12]Learn from the history of successful battles.
Victory goes to those who make winning easy.
A good battle is one that you will obviously win.
It doesn't take intelligence to win a reputation.
It doesn't take courage to achieve success.

[17]You must win your battles without effort.
Avoid difficult struggles.
Fight when your position must win.
You always win by preventing your defeat.

[21]You must engage only in winning battles.
Position yourself where you cannot lose.
Never waste an opportunity to defeat your enemy.

[24]You win a war by first assuring yourself of victory.
Only afterward do you look for a fight.
Outmaneuver the enemy before the first battle and then
fight to win.

We must constantly be looking for easy situations in which we can hurt terrorists and their supporters with very little risk to ourselves. We must win small confrontation after small confrontation easily. Our goals should be so easily accomplished that the press ignores them. Our long-term success requires playing it safe.

Despite the media's efforts to portray our invasion of Iraq as difficult, that attack remains the easiest battle of its size in human history. We knew that we would win and, more importantly, our opponents were just as certain that they could not stop us.

We must make it clear that we are actively committed to similar battles. If the Baathists in Syria give us cause, they must know that our position in Iraq makes displacing them even easier.

Before we go after other states supporting terrorism, we must make Iraq a success that demonstrates our intentions to help the local people. If Muslims know that they will directly benefit from our intervention, we will win these battles before they begin.

You must make good use of war. 4
Study military philosophy and the art of defense.
You can control your victory or defeat.

4This is the art of war:
"1.   Discuss the distances.
2.   Discuss your numbers.
3.   Discuss your calculations.
4.   Discuss your decisions.
5.   Discuss victory.

10The ground determines the distance.
The distance determines your numbers.
Your numbers determine your calculations.
Your calculations determine your decisions.
Your decisions determine your victory."

15Creating a winning war is like balancing a coin of gold
against a coin of silver.
Creating a losing war is like balancing a coin of silver
against a coin of gold.

Winning a battle is always a matter of people. 5
You pour them into battle like a flood of water pouring into
a deep gorge.
This is a matter of positioning.

♦ ♦ ♦

4 We must use the strong position that we have established in the Middle East. We must protect our people there and use our presence there to find new ways to win against terrorism.

A strong presence in Iraq and Afghanistan puts our forces right on the borders of the states that encourage terrorism. We have enough forces in the area to create military superiority in a number of operations throughout the area. Most of those operations against terrorists can and should go unnoticed in the press, but it is those activities that gradually whittle down terrorist organizations.

Without a position in Iraq and Afghanistan, we would be too distant to threaten the terrorist organizations rooted in that part of the world. We would be severely limited in terms of the forces available in that region. With a position in Iraq and Afghanistan, we have more options that create the potential for victory.

As long as we had a limited position in the Middle East, our enemies could choose situations in which they could easily hurt us. We have now turned that situation around; no one in that area thinks that we lack either the will or the resources to defeat them.

5 Our success depends upon what the people in the Muslim world choose for themselves. They have seen the Islamic states of the Taliban and the Iranian mullahs. We now must demonstrate the power of freedom and opportunity in Iraq and Afghanistan.

Chapter 5

Momentum: Innovation against Terror

Momentum means putting people and events in motion in such a way that they become unstoppable. What interests Sun Tzu is how momentum is created by systematic innovation that combines traditional methods with new approaches.

For a long period of time, the terrorists had all the momentum in their battle for recognition. In 1979, the attack on the US embassy in Iran increased support for fundamentalism within the Muslim community. Terrorists realized the value of this new technique in 1983 when they started a series of embassy bombings. At first these were military attacks on embassies or troops, but by 1984 terrorists had discovered that attacks on airliners worked as well and were even more highly publicized. They soon expanded to all types of civilian targets—cruise ships, discotheques, hotels, buses, etc. This trend peaked with the explosion of a 747 over Lockerbie, Scotland. Subsequent attacks on civilian buildings followed, culminating on 9/11.

We seized back the momentum after 9/11 in Afghanistan and Iraq. However, our military victories are not enough. This is what the world expects of the United States. We must do something that no one expects. We must add a spiritual message to our military victories that resonates within Islamic culture. Right now, the terrorists claim the spiritual high ground; we must actively work to take this away from them. We can maintain our momentum through a religious message that supports our military success.

Momentum

SUN TZU SAID:

You control a large group the same as you control a few. 1
You just divide their ranks correctly.
You fight a large army the same as you fight a small one.
You only need the right position and communication.
You may meet a large enemy army.
You must be able to sustain an enemy attack without being
defeated.
You must correctly use both surprise and direct action.
Your army's position must increase your strength.
Troops flanking an enemy can smash them like eggs.
You must correctly use both strength and weakness.

It is the same in all battles. 2
You use a direct approach to engage the enemy.
You use surprise to win.

4You must use surprise for a successful invasion.
Surprise is as infinite as the weather and land.
Surprise is as inexhaustible as the flow of a river.

Innovation against Terror

1 Terrorist organizations may be large and spread throughout the world, but we can tackle them one at a time. Our strategy against terror must break up the terrorists' web of alliances. This demands a strong stance against terror and good communication among the various states fighting terror. Terror attacks are painful for those who care about human life, but even the terrorists' worst attacks cannot destroy our society or way of life.

We must use both innovative and proven methods in our fight. Our position in the world must keep terrorists on the defensive. We can prove that the terrorists' claims of divine support are hollow by pitting our strengths against their weaknesses.

2 The War on Terror is like every other war. We must directly challenge the terrorists by meeting them in battle, but we must use what they don't expect—the Muslim religion—to truly defeat them.

We surprised the terrorists by invading the Middle East. We can shock them by leveraging Islamic culture and history against them. In Islamic culture, we must side with the will of God.

7You can be stopped and yet recover the initiative.
You must use your days and months correctly.

9If you are defeated, you can recover.
You must use the four seasons correctly.

11There are only a few notes in the scale.
Yet you can always rearrange them.
You can never hear every song of victory.

14There are only a few basic colors.
Yet you can always mix them.
You can never see all the shades of victory.

17There are only a few flavors.
Yet you can always blend them.
You can never taste all the flavors of victory.

20You fight with momentum.
There are only a few types of surprises and direct actions.
Yet you can always vary the ones you use.
There is no limit to the ways you can win.

24Surprise and direct action give birth to each other.
They are like a circle without end.
You cannot exhaust all their possible combinations!

Surging water flows together rapidly. 3
Its pressure washes away boulders.
This is momentum.

Even though the terrorists will have successful attacks in the future, we cannot let them claim that their success is God's will.

We can quickly recover from a devastating terrorist attack, productively using the years that follow to prove that our system is resilient.

A simple-sounding message that individual freedom of choice is a gift from God can be powerful in Muslim countries because Islam requires individuals to freely submit to the will of God.

People form their opinions based on what they see. To win the War on Terror, we cannot wallow in every Satanic image of individual freedom while censoring the Satanic images of terrorism.

In the end, individuals know what they like. Muslims have many different spiritual tastes. They don't have to agree on what Islam is to know that the personal freedom to pursue God is good.

We need to build up momentum in this War on Terror. We must add this strong spiritual message to our superior military abilities. We must change our traditional moral justifications for this special war. We need not limit ourselves to a secular defense of freedom.

This spiritual dimension supports our military actions. Military victories come from God. We can dedicate them to God. For Muslims and traditional Americans, this is an unbeatable combination.

3 Constant pressure and quick action are the keys to momentum. Water is Sun Tzu's metaphor for change. By continually refining our message, we keep the momentum in the battle against terror.

⁴A hawk suddenly strikes a bird.
Its contact alone kills the prey.
This is timing.

⁷You must fight only winning battles.
Your momentum must be overwhelming.
Your timing must be exact.

¹⁰Your momentum is like the tension of a bent crossbow.
Your timing is like the pulling of a trigger.

War is very complicated and confusing. 4
Battle is chaotic.
Nevertheless, you must not allow chaos.

⁴War is very sloppy and messy.
Positions turn around.
Nevertheless, you must never be defeated.

⁷Chaos gives birth to control.
Fear gives birth to courage.
Weakness gives birth to strength.

¹⁰You must control chaos.
This depends on your planning.
Your men must brave their fears.
This depends on their momentum.

¹⁴You have strengths and weaknesses.
These come from your position.

We must learn how to strike unexpectedly. Both our military and our message must be more flexible so both can be deployed to new targets quickly. We must act on new information instantly.

Our success depends on constantly making progress against terror. Everyone, especially in the media, should see who is winning. We can control the timing of both our battles and our messages.

Our momentum pressures terrorist organizations. A strong Islamic message must explain the tension that our victories create.

4 No war is predictable, and the hidden nature of terrorism makes this war particularly chaotic. We can never forget that this is a media war, so we must always explain what is happening.

We are going to make mistakes in this war. We are going to be caught off guard. Our mistakes will be trumpeted in the media, but we cannot be discouraged or deterred in our mission.

The unpredictability of terrorists must increase our vigilance. We must use the fear of a terror attack as motivation. Our freedom and faith are both our greatest weaknesses and greatest strengths.

We can minimize chaos by planning both our military responses and responses communicating our spiritual message. By maintaining the momentum in this battle, Americans have less to fear and can be confident in success.

The position we take both on the physical battlefield and on the media battlefield determines how we can attack and be attacked.

¹⁶You must force the enemy to move to your advantage.

Use your position.

The enemy must follow you.

Surrender a position.

The enemy must take it.

You can offer an advantage to move him.

You can use your men to move him.

You can use your strength to hold him.

You want a successful battle. 5

To do this, you must seek momentum.

Do not just demand a good fight from your people.

You must pick good people and then give them momentum.

⁵You must create momentum.

You create it with your men during battle.

This is comparable to rolling trees and stones.

Trees and stones roll because of their shape and weight.

Offer men safety and they will stay calm.

Endanger them and they will act.

Give them a place and they will hold.

Round them up and they will march.

¹³You make your men powerful in battle with momentum.

This should be like rolling round stones down over a high,

steep cliff.

Momentum is critical.

We can reposition the terrorists both on the physical battle-field and in the media war. When we establish a position in Iraq and Afghanistan, we force the terrorists to confront us there. If we distance ourselves from tyrants in the Islamic world, we force the terrorists to ally themselves with tyrants. We can offer the terrorists appealing targets to draw them out of hiding. We can push them around with our military strength. We can leverage our strength to hold down their numbers and limit their financial capabilities.

5 We must meet the challenges of terrorism by building our momentum in both the physical and psychological war. We cannot simply ask that our defenders work hard to protect us. We must pick leaders who can sustain our momentum in this battle.

To sustain momentum, we must continually surprise our opponents. This depends on using our people wisely. People naturally follow the path of least resistance. Good leaders harness our natural reactions to threats. They maintain our confidence that they can defend us against terror, but we must feel the danger so that we are willing to continue the fight. Our leaders must put us in positions that we will readily defend. These positions must unite us so that we can work together against the threat.

We can gain power not only in the Middle East but worldwide by further establishing our momentum. People can't stop a focused force for change. America has long been a force for change in the world; this war just continues that historical tradition.

Chapter 6

Weakness and Strength: The Terrorists' Weak Points

This chapter takes us more deeply into Sun Tzu's underlying strategic concepts. The two opposing and complementary ideas of weakness and strength presented in this chapter describe the mechanism by which we avoid difficult battles and turn problems into opportunities. In strategic analysis, these two seemingly opposite ideas are bound together. Not only does an opponent's weakness create our strengths, but our strengths can also be our weaknesses. Every battlefield has both strong points and weak points. Each creates the other.

Science says that nature abhors a vacuum. Similarly, strategic science teaches that openings invite competitors to fill them. These openings can be in the marketplace of ideas or on a physical battlefield. Terrorists discovered, perhaps accidentally, that militarily senseless attacks could win them free advertising in the marketplace of ideas. In Sun Tzu's terms, by arriving first on this particular battlefield, the terrorists found a key weakness in modern society.

Sun Tzu explains that there is a strict relationship between our knowledge (and ignorance) and our strengths (and weaknesses). We must know enough about the terrorists in order to understand their weaknesses. Secrecy creates opportunities to exploit the terrorists' weaknesses. Every idea covered thus far in *The Art of War*—planning, using people, positioning, and meeting challenges—can be related directly to leveraging the terrorists' weaknesses against them.

Weakness and Strength

SUN TZU SAID:

Always arrive first to the empty battlefield to await the 1
enemy at your leisure.
After the battleground is occupied and you hurry to it,
fighting is more difficult.

3You want a successful battle.
Move your men, but not into opposing forces.

5You can make the enemy come to you.
Offer him an advantage.
You can make the enemy avoid coming to you.
Threaten him with danger.

9When the enemy is fresh, you can tire him.
When he is well fed, you can starve him.
When he is relaxed, you can move him.

The Terrorists' Weak Points

1 Strategically, a battlefield is any place where two competitors meet. On the media battlefield, terrorism offers a fresh story.
Murderers are common, but religious fanatics who practice suicidal
murders are new, exciting, and interesting to the media.

Through the media, the terrorists found an opening into a world
dominated by American cultural, economic, and military power.

Increased donations and recruitment rewarded acts of terror on
civilian targets, so terrorists found more and bigger targets. After
we withdrew from Lebanon and later Somalia, the terrorists saw
that there was little risk that they would be punished for their acts.

But the newness of terror is gone. The rewards won from terror are
more costly. Because the terrorists were confident that they were
safe, Americans could push them out of Afghanistan and Iraq.

Leave any place without haste. 2
Hurry to where you are unexpected.
You can easily march hundreds of miles without tiring.
To do so, travel through areas that are deserted.
You must take whatever you attack.
Attack when there is no defense.
You must have walls to defend.
Defend where it is impossible to attack.

⁹Be skilled in attacking.
Give the enemy no idea where to defend.

¹¹Be skillful in your defense.
Give the enemy no idea where to attack.

Be subtle! Be subtle! 3
Arrive without any clear formation.
Ghostly! Ghostly!
Arrive without a sound.
You must use all your skill to control the enemy's decisions.

⁶Advance where he can't defend.
Charge through his openings.
Withdraw where the enemy cannot chase you.
Move quickly so that he cannot catch you.

2 Before 9/11, terrorists didn't have to worry about rushing their attacks. They could strike quickly wherever they found an opportunity. They could move quickly from one area of the world to another because no one was actively opposing them. They could pick civilian targets where their success was certain because few of their targets were actively defended. They could hide in states that supported terror, knowing that they were protected from international law enforcement by the power of a friendly state.

Since they could (and still can) attack millions of possible targets, no one could defend against them.

The terrorists thought that they were protected by international borders. Their camps in Afghanistan were open to our attacks.

3 Terrorist organizations are secret societies. Their structure is hidden. They are sheltered within a world of kinship and clans. They are mysterious and threatening. They move into new areas and select their targets without advertising their presence. They thought that they understood America and how we would react.

The terrorists thought that they would always have safe targets. They thought that they could keep surprising us. The planners and leaders of terror thought that they could always stay one step ahead of those who wanted to bring them to justice.

¹⁰Always pick your own battles.
The enemy can hide behind high walls and deep trenches.
Do not try to win by fighting him directly.
Instead, attack a place that he must recapture.
Avoid the battles that you don't want.
You can divide the ground and yet defend it.
Don't give the enemy anything to win.
Divert him from coming to where you defend.

Make other men take a position while you take none. 4
Then focus your forces where the enemy divides his forces.
Where you focus, you unite your forces.
When the enemy divides, he creates many small groups.
You want your large group to attack one of his small ones.
Then you have many men where the enemy has but a few.
Your larger force can overwhelm his smaller one.
Then go on to the next small enemy group.
You can take them one at a time.

You must keep the place that you have chosen as a 5
battleground a secret.
The enemy must not know.
Force the enemy to prepare his defense in many places.
You want the enemy to defend many places.
Then you can choose where to fight.
His forces will be weak there.

After 9/11, America began choosing the battlegrounds. Terrorist leaders thought they were protected, but we didn't go after them directly. Instead we went after the regimes that sheltered them. This brought the terrorists out in the open. Controlling the ground, we now pick when and where to fight. We have forced countries in the Middle East to fight terror. Terrorists can still kill, but their activity is less newsworthy. Killing is common in a hot war. Most importantly, we are now fighting the terrorists there instead of here.

4 Now that we have established a strong position in the Middle East, the loose network organization of terrorism, once its strength, is now its weakness. Terrorists are naturally divided. In a hot war, their lack of hierarchy works against them. Killing them is still a dangerous job, but small groups of terrorists are dealt with one at a time as we organize the forces needed to eliminate them. In every confrontation, we control the balance of forces. After dealing with one group in one area, we can move on to the next group in the next area. We can work through terrorist hot spots one at a time.

5 When we are just waiting for terrorist attacks, we are at a disadvantage because we don't know where the attacks will come. Our ignorance of the intended targets is our weakness. We are forced to defend many different types of targets, but the terrorists know that we cannot defend everywhere. By diluting our defenses, we leave openings and weaknesses. Terrorists can find and exploit those weaknesses.

⁷If he reinforces his front lines, he depletes his rear.
If he reinforces his rear, he depletes his front.
If he reinforces his right flank, he depletes his left.
If he reinforces his left flank, he depletes his right.
Without knowing the place of attack, he cannot prepare.
Without knowing the right place, he will be weak everywhere.

¹³The enemy has weak points.
Prepare your men against them.
He has strong points.
Make his men prepare themselves against you.

You must know the battleground. 6
You must know the time of battle.
You can then travel a thousand miles and still win the battle.

⁴The enemy should not know the battleground.
He shouldn't know the time of battle.
His left flank will be unable to support his right.
His right will be unable to support his left.
His front lines will be unable to support his rear.
His rear will be unable to support his front.
His support is distant even if it is only ten miles away.
What unknown place can be close?

¹²You control the balance of forces.
The enemy may have many men but they are superfluous.
How can they help him to victory?

We cannot defend ourselves from terror by shifting resources from one area to another. We do not have infinite resources and have to prioritize their use. We put more resources into airline security, but we cannot put the same effort into protecting water reservoirs. Terrorists can always find a soft target to attack. This is why Sun Tzu teaches that the best defense is a good offense.

The terrorists cannot afford direct confrontations. By fighting them in Iraq and Afghanistan, we consume their limited resources. Terrorists now have to worry about defending their strongholds in Syria and Iran. How safe are they in those countries?

6 Who chooses the time and place of battle? If the terrorists decide, they target our weaknesses. If we decide, we can successfully target the terrorists' assets, even at a great distance.

In an asymmetric war, terrorists can successfully keep their secrets. The press cannot or—when Al Jazeera is given foreknowledge of an attack, for example, so its journalists can photograph it—will not report terrorist plans. Keeping secrets is much more difficult in America. The media can and will report every movement our military makes. Media analysts try to spot our weaknesses so they can report them. Even when our operations are successful, the media will report on every unavoidable problem so they can criticize it.

Despite our problems with keeping secrets from the media, we can still control the balance of forces. Our real-time transportation and communications are far superior.

¹⁵We say:
You must let victory happen.

¹⁷The enemy may have many men.
You can still control him without a fight.

When you form your strategy, know the strengths and 7
weaknesses of your plan.
When you execute a plan, know how to manage both action
and inaction.
When you take a position, know the deadly and the winning
grounds.
When you enter into battle, know when you have too many
or too few men.

⁵Use your position as your war's centerpiece.
Arrive at the battle without a formation.
Don't take a position in advance.
Then even the best spies can't report it.
Even the wisest general cannot plan to counter you.
Take a position where you can triumph using superior numbers.
Keep opposing forces ignorant.
Everyone should learn your location after your position has
given you success.
No one should know how your location gives you a winning
position.
Make a successful battle one from which the enemy cannot
recover.
You must continually adjust your position to his position.

We must be opportunistic in fighting terrorists. We must use what opportunities the terrorists give us to attack and kill them.

In the end, we will not have to fight everyone who supports terror because, knowing they will die, most will choose not to fight.

7 In planning our War on Terror, we must focus on what we can know rather than what we cannot know. Our knowledge is never perfect, but we still have to act. In executing our war, we must know when to press the fight and when to wait for a better opportunity. It is always better to fight terrorists in their own land rather than trying to defend against attacks here. We must control the time and place of battle so that we also have a clear superiority of forces when we confront the terrorists.

The military positions that we have established in Iraq and Afghanistan are our biggest strengths in this war. The terrorists are now at a disadvantage because they can't know where we are going next. Is Iran a target? Is Syria? Because we haven't committed to a course of action, the press cannot report it. The leaders in Iran and Syria know that we could overpower them, and that worries them and encourages their opponents. As long as these leaders feel threatened, they will be careful about giving us a reason to attack them.

We should start using this position in the Middle East to work *secretly* with those who oppose terror and against those who support terror. We can and should support the groups in the region that are willing to fight for freedom and democracy. We should make it clear that we are relentless and that the days are numbered for terrorist organizations and the states that support them.

Manage your military position like water. 8
Water takes every shape.
It avoids the high and moves to the low.
Your war can take any shape.
It must avoid the strong and strike the weak.
Water follows the shape of the land that directs its flow.
Your forces follow the enemy, who determines how you win.

[8]Make war without a standard approach.
Water has no consistent shape.
If you follow the enemy's shifts and changes, you can always
find a way to win.
We call this shadowing.

[12]Fight five different campaigns without a firm rule for victory.
Use all four seasons without a consistent position.
Your timing must be sudden.
A few weeks determine your failure or success.

✦ ✦ ✦

8 We cannot defend rigid positions, such as protecting Middle Eastern civilian centers where the terrorists can find easy targets and we will get the blame. Strategy means leveraging the forces of change, not fighting to hold them back. We must make civilians responsible for protecting themselves, committing to help them when the terrorists try to amass a serious force. We must constantly advance our position, moving into the terrorists' weak points.

The problemwith large bureaucracies, military or otherwise, is that they are predictable. Good strategy requires that we continually change our position to undermine the terrorists' attempts to establish a stronger position. If we continually change the situation, we will eventually discover an opportunity to destroy them.

Different situations require different approaches. Only the media and the terrorists want our forces to act predictably. When we act, we must learn to move more quickly. Our opportunities to catch terrorists can vanish overnight.

✦ ✦ ✦

Chapter 7

Armed Conflict: Minimizing Destruction

In this chapter, Sun Tzu covers the rules for avoiding or engaging in deadly conflict. This war is about more than killing terrorists. We must defeat terrorism in such a way that others become disenchanted with terror. In fighting a psychological war, we have to structure direct engagements so that we always win. In coming to fight us in Iraq or Afghanistan, the terrorists are making the strategic error of looking for armed conflict.

Our message must be that America wins because we fight for God. No true Muslim believes that any nation, no matter how strong, can stand against the will of Allah. If we keep winning, it is because Allah wants us to win. The terrorists will try to frame our victories in their favor. They will say that they are losing because Allah is unhappy that more Muslims are not joining the cause. As Sun Tzu makes clear in this chapter, winning isn't enough. A large part of our job is communication.

Strategically, we cannot react predictably in confronting terrorism. In transitions, such as turning over power in Iraq, we must surprise the terrorists. Sun Tzu's ideas suggest some strategic options that we can easily overlook in fighting terror and that we should probably pursue.

The chapter ends with an explanation of how we control the emotions that tend to dominate violent confrontations. By controlling those emotions we can minimize destruction and dramatically improve our position.

Armed Conflict

SUN TZU SAID:

Everyone uses the arts of war. 1
You accept orders from the government.
Then you assemble your army.
You organize your men and build camps.
You must avoid disasters from armed conflict.

[6]Seeking armed conflict can be disastrous.
Because of this, a detour can be the shortest path.
Because of this, problems can become opportunities.

[9]Use an indirect route as your highway.
Use the search for advantage to guide you.
When you fall behind, you must catch up.
When you get ahead, you must wait.
You must know the detour that most directly accomplishes
your plan.

[14]Undertake armed conflict when you have an advantage.
Seeking armed conflict for its own sake is dangerous.

Minimizing Destruction

1 America and the terrorists are both bound by the same laws of strategy. We both get direction from our leaders. We are both building up our forces. We both have to organize and train our people. And, especially since this is a media war, both sides have to avoid confrontations that can destroy their men and resources.

The terrorists have tried to avoid fighting military battles because they know they will lose, but America, with its military superiority, must also find success by avoiding worthless battles.

In the invasion of Iraq, we avoided most cities and the dangerous street fights within them. We moved through weaknesses in the Iraqi lines. When we encountered resistance in one area, we shifted resources elsewhere. Advance forces waited for the main forces to catch up. Despite the constant criticism in the press, the military minimized casualties on both sides.

We fought directly only when our technological superiority made success with a minimum of casualties absolutely certain.

You can build up an army to fight for an advantage. 2
Then you won't catch the enemy.
You can force your army to go fight for an advantage.
Then you abandon your heavy supply wagons.

5You keep only your armor and hurry after the enemy.
You avoid stopping day or night.
You use many roads at the same time.
You go hundreds of miles to fight for an advantage.
Then the enemy catches your commanders and your army.
Your strong soldiers get there first.
Your weaker soldiers follow behind.
Using this approach, only one in ten will arrive.
You can try to go fifty miles to fight for an advantage.
Then your commanders and army will stumble.
Using this method, only half of your soldiers will make it.
You can try to go thirty miles to fight for an advantage.
Then only two out of three will get there.

18If you make your army travel without good supply lines,
your army will die.
Without supplies and food, your army will die.
If you don't save the harvest, your army will die.

2 The reaction of the terrorists after the American victory in Iraq shows why they cannot afford to seek direct confrontation. In flooding into Iraq to fight the Americans, the terrorists abandoned their support networks within their local Muslim communities.

In rushing to fight the Americans, the terrorists came to Iraq from throughout the Middle East without resources. They travelled into unfamiliar territory, coming from many different regions. They found themselves on uncertain ground in a country that considered them foreigners. Soon after they began to arrive, the symbol of American opposition, Saddam, was captured. The most aggressive terrorists came first, but they were separated from their less dedicated followers and had no connection to local fighters.

Over time, terrorism becomes more localized. In Iraq, secondary leaders such as Moqtada al-Sadr have arisen but they make a mistake when they seek conflict with the Americans. Eventually, terrorists will stay closer to home, attacking their own communities. More will survive, but they sacrifice local support and limited resources.

Over time, terrorists must realize that they need supporters within the Islamic community to survive. Outside terrorists cannot operate with limited resources and ammunition. They cannot continue to fight without a financial and intelligence support network.

²¹Do not let any of your potential enemies know what you
are planning.

Still, you must not hesitate to form alliances.

You must know the mountains and forests.

You must know where the obstructions are.

You must know where the marshes are.

If you don't, you cannot move the army.

If you don't, you must use local guides.

If you don't, you can't take advantage of the terrain.

You make war by making a false stand. 3

By finding an advantage, you can move.

By dividing and joining, you can reinvent yourself and transform the situation.

You can move as quickly as the wind.

You can rise like the forest.

You can invade and plunder like fire.

You can stay as motionless as a mountain.

You can be as mysterious as the fog.

You can strike like sounding thunder.

¹⁰Divide your troops to plunder the villages.

When on open ground, dividing is an advantage.

Don't worry about organization; just move.

Be the first to find a new route that leads directly to a winning plan.

This is how you are successful at armed conflict.

America recovered from a strategic error in announcing the turnover date in Iraq by turning over sovereignty early. We must continue to build ties with local supporters throughout the region. Local groups know where the terrorists can hide and seek refuge. They know the people who oppose personal freedom in the Islamic world. Our allies can tell us where we could get bogged down on uncertain ground. Without this local knowledge, we cannot continue to make progress in the Middle East. Without local supporters we can trust, we cannot use our position in Iraq well.

3 America doesn't have to do what is expected. We can move our troops where they are needed. We can reposition ourselves using the divisions in the Muslim world to transform the situation. We can choose to reenter the fight when antiterrorist forces need our support. We can leverage shifts in the economic climate. We can set up strong defensive positions that cannot be challenged. If terrorists build support in an area, we can invade that area and punish its people. A strong presence doesn't require much action. We should keep everyone guessing about what we will do next. We can shape events to dominate the media when we want to.

From bases in Iraq and Afghanistan, we can raid terrorist camps in Syria and Iran. Avoiding Syrian and Iranian armies, we can strike many places at once. We can't afford to worry about diplomacy; we need to move. We have to try different techniques and find new ways to defeat terrorists and their supporters. This is how we minimize the long-term destruction of the war.

Military experience says: 4
"You can speak, but you will not be heard.
You must use gongs and drums.
You cannot really see your forces just by looking.
You must use banners and flags."

⁶You must master gongs, drums, banners, and flags.
Place people as a single unit where they can all see and hear.
You must unite them as one.
Then the brave cannot advance alone.
The fearful cannot withdraw alone.
You must force them to act as a group.

¹²In night battles, you must use numerous fires and drums.
In day battles, you must use many banners and flags.
You must position your people to control what they see and
hear.

You control your army by controlling its morale. 5
As a general, you must be able to control emotions.

³In the morning, a person's energy is high.
During the day, it fades.
By evening, a person's thoughts turn to home.
You must use your troops wisely.
Avoid the enemy's high spirits.
Strike when his men are lazy and want to go home.
This is how you master energy.

4 America can never forget that this is a media war. This doesn't mean just sending a message. It means being heard. We must make serious investments in projects such as the Iraqi Media Network, composed of six television stations and three radio stations. We need greater influence over what Muslim people hear and see.

The goal of Middle East ground control should be exposing the Muslims to the unifying message of freedom and prosperity. This communication can consolidate those who support dramatic, historical reforms in the region. Without media to support this view, the brave champions of reform cannot advance their position. With a positive media, even those who are afraid can begin to speak out.

When there is confusion, we should increase our communication in the area. We should create visible symbols for the idea of increasing economic freedom. We want everyone, even those in the most remote areas, to be given a positive vision of their future.

5 We will win this war by leveraging the emotions of journalists, the terrorists, the American people, and the Muslim world.

Controlling emotion through the media is largely a matter of timing. Emotion is the highest immediately after an event. Americans have a notoriously short attention span. We must act quickly after events that work in our favor, providing people a positive outlet for their emotion. Terrorists set up celebrations after successful terrorist attacks. We can use these same acts to stage events to build support against terror. We must harness people's energy.

¹⁰Use discipline to await the chaos of battle.
Keep relaxed to await a crisis.
This is how you master emotion.

¹³Stay close to home to await the distant enemy.
Stay comfortable to await the weary enemy.
Stay well fed to await the hungry enemy.
This is how you master power.

Don't entice the enemy when his ranks are orderly.
You must not attack when his formations are solid.
This is how you master adaptation.

⁴You must follow these military rules.
Do not take a position facing the high ground.
Do not oppose those with their backs to the wall.
Do not follow those who pretend to flee.
Do not attack the enemy's strongest men.
Do not swallow the enemy's bait.
Do not block an army that is heading home.
Leave an escape outlet for a surrounded army.
Do not press a desperate foe.
This is how you use military skills.

✦ ✦ ✦

We must show discipline while awaiting a successful terrorist attack. We should prepare people for these attacks so they don't panic. Through preparation we control emotional reactions.

The best way to prepare for a terrorist attack is to further build up our economy. We can stay comfortable while we make the terrorists uncomfortable. We can stay economically strong while starving terrorist organizations. This is how we stay powerful.

6 We cannot leave easy targets for the terrorists when they are organizing to act. We must not attack terrorists and their supporters without first dividing them. We must adapt to the conditions.

Our goal is to strengthen our position, not merely kill people. We should never give terrorists the high moral or religious ground. We should always give terrorists the option of giving up rather than dying, but we shouldn't be taken in by false concessions. We shouldn't chase after terrorists into areas where their support is strongest. We cannot accept the terrorists' reasoning. We should always encourage the terrorists to go home and lead normal lives. When we trap a group of terrorists, we should allow them a way to give up honorably. We don't want to force them into a mass suicide. This is how we minimize destruction.

Chapter 8

Adaptability: Shifting Our Priorities

It is hard to change. People tend to keep doing what has worked in the past. If we are going to be successful in fighting terror, we are going to have to adapt to the evolving situation more quickly than the terrorists do.

As our position changes, we must adjust to the new realities of our situation. We now have a substantial physical presence in the Middle East. This fact changes everything. Our new position creates new problems. It also creates new opportunities. This new position requires new strategies.

The faster we adapt to our new position in the Middle East, the more successful we will be. We are no longer outsiders. We have a place, probably a long-term one, in that part of the world. We must change the way we think to solve the problems we will face.

We have a large military force in the Middle East, but we do not have political stability. The coalition army won the territory, so our temptation is to keep using the army to police it. But using an occupying army to win the hearts and minds of local people is like using a stick of dynamite to open a letter. It is the type of strategic mistake that Sun Tzu warns about in this chapter. New situations demand new strategies, new weapons, and fresh ideas.

Our army won us the new position. We must trust that new position to supply the new tools we need to stabilize that situation. The most powerful tool is the hopes and aspirations of the local people themselves.

Adaptability

SUN TZU SAID:

Everyone uses the arts of war. 1
As a general, you get your orders from the government.
You gather your troops.
On dangerous ground, you must not camp.
Where the roads intersect, you must join your allies.
When an area is cut off, you must not delay in it.
When you are surrounded, you must scheme.
In a life-or-death situation, you must fight.
There are roads that you must not take.
There are armies that you must not fight.
There are strongholds that you must not attack.
There are positions that you must not defend.
There are government commands that must not be obeyed.

[14]Military leaders must be experts in knowing how to adapt
to find an advantage.
This will teach you the use of war.

[16]Some commanders are not good at making adjustments to
find an advantage.
They can know the shape of the terrain.
Still, they cannot find an advantageous position.

Shifting Our Priorities

1 We naturally to go through certain steps in organizing a military effort. During this period, we can control what we do. This control, however, is inherently limited. Once we engage the enemy, we can no longer freely choose what we do or don't do. Most of our actions are dictated by our specific situation in the field. Here the list of specific situations—dangerous ground, intersecting roads, cut-off areas, etc.—is a sampling of the much more detailed lists in the following three chapters. Despite our victories in Iraq and Afghanistan, it is not safe or wise for us to go many places in those countries. We cannot get involved in many fights between local factions. There are places, such as holy shrines, that we may not want to attack. We must resist the temptation to do what is impossible, no matter what politicians say or the media demands.

We must be free to adapt our techniques to counter what each new situation requires. This is especially true as we seek to stabilize the situation in Iraq and Afghanistan.

At this stage of the War on Terror, our challenge is using our forces to maximize our opportunities to undermine terrorism. We want to use our troops to provide law enforcement and rebuilding because we know it is needed, but this is not what we do best.

[19]Some military commanders do not know how to adjust
their methods.
They can find an advantageous position.
Still, they cannot use their men effectively.

You must be creative in your planning. 2
You must adapt to your opportunities and weaknesses.
You can use a variety of approaches and still have a consis-
tent result.
You must adjust to a variety of problems and consistently
solve them.

You can deter your potential enemy by using his 3
weaknesses against him.
You can keep your potential enemy's army busy by giving it
work to do.
You can rush your potential enemy by offering him an
advantageous position.

You must make use of war. 4
Do not trust that the enemy isn't coming.
Trust your readiness to meet him.
Do not trust that the enemy won't attack.
Rely only on your ability to pick a place that the enemy can't
attack.

When the United States moved into the Middle East, the terrorists needed to change their methods, but they were trapped by their rhetoric. After years of preaching against the Great Satan, they cannot resist fruitless attacks when Satan is in their backyard.

2 We must be more creative than the terrorists. We want to rebuild the Middle East, but that is our weakness. Free enterprise is a more powerful weapon than an army in creating wealth and political support. The local people will take the necessary risks if they know there are firm rules for winning rewards. Market incentives can solve more problems than military might can.

3 The weakness of the terrorists is that they cannot offer their supporters any future other than death. By promoting economic freedom in the Middle East, we can give potential terrorist recruits productive work to do, building a life for themselves. We can entice the terrorists to overplay their hand by acting against the best interests of the local people in attacking these rebuilding projects.

4 We will win this war by good strategy, not by force. We can be assured that the terrorists want to destroy us. We have to be ready to meet their challenge. The terrorists are certain to try to attack us. It is better that they target our soldiers in the Middle East rather than our civilians here. Our job is establishing a position in those countries that the terrorists find impossible to effectively attack.

You can exploit five different faults in a leader.
If he is willing to die, you can kill him.
If he wants to survive, you can capture him.
He may have a quick temper.
You can then provoke him with insults.
If he has a delicate sense of honor, you can disgrace him.
If he loves his people, you can create problems for him.
In every situation, look for these five weaknesses.
They are common faults in commanders.
They always lead to military disaster.

[11]To overturn an army, you must kill its general.
To do this, you must use these five weaknesses.
You must always look for them.

5 The key to destroying Islamic terrorism is to undermine its leaders. We cannot be shy about killing leaders, such as bin Laden, who are willing to die. Others, such as Saddam, we are better off capturing. But even if we cannot kill or capture them, we can provoke them by drawing attention to their cowardice and weakness. We can insult their intelligence and point out their hypocrisy. We can expose the duplicity and corruption of their friends and supporters, even in the UN and France. The American government is often too diplomatic. We tend to ignore terrorist leaders rather than demonize them. We have to remember that this is a media war.

To destroy a movement such as Islamic terrorism, we must discredit its leaders. They are not icons. The more people know about them, the less likely people are to respect them.

✦ ✦ ✦

Chapter 9

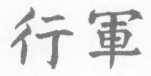 

Armed March: Campaigning against Terror

The campaign against terror is both a physical war and a psychological war. This long chapter discusses four different types of environments and how we utilize them in our War on Terror. These environments are physical for the soldiers in the field, social within Middle Eastern society, and psychological in the larger media war.

This chapter is both a prescription for and a prediction about how the fight will progress in our battle against terrorism. We must deal with divisions within the Muslim world, channel the pressures for change, and weather the uncertainties inherent in this task. We can win the war against terror if we leverage the asymmetric nature of the battlefield that dramatically favors some positions over others.

We must meet terrorist forces on the ground, undermine their organizations within Muslim society, and destroy their image in the media war. To accomplish these three tasks successfully, we must foresee the shape that the battle will take over time. Sun Tzu offers a detailed preview of the various changes that terrorist organizations will go through as they find it more and more difficult to operate and rebuild.

The chapter ends by discussing the difficulties encountered in developing new democratic societies. The two political traditions of the Muslim world—national socialism and Islamic fundamentalism—have poorly equipped the people in the region with the skills required to build democracy. We must make it easy for them to master those skills.

Armed March

SUN TZU SAID:

Anyone moving an army must adjust to the enemy. 1
When caught in the mountains, rely on their valleys.
Position yourself on the heights facing the sun.
To win your battles, never attack uphill.
This is how you position your army in the mountains.

⁶When water blocks you, keep far away from it.
Let the invader cross the river and wait for him.
Do not meet him in midstream.
Wait for him to get half his forces across and then take
advantage of the situation.

¹⁰You need to be able to fight.
You can't do that if you are caught in water when you meet
an invader.
Position yourself upstream, facing the sun.
Never face against the current.
Always position your army upstream when near the water.

Campaigning against Terror

1 To make progress against terror, we must keep pressuring the terrorists. When we meet them in environments such as Middle Eastern society or the mainstream media, which are very unequal, America must take the high ground. We can't directly attack the prejudices of those environments but have to work with them.

Water represents the chaotic forces of change. When turmoil engulfs the area—if a revolution breaks out in Syria, or the battle between Israel and Palestine heats up—we must initially stay out of it. We must let the terrorists get involved in these disputes first so that we can then attack them, taking advantage of the situation.

We must stay focused on our true enemies, the Islamic fascists who are at war with America. We cannot do this if we get trapped in other conflicts in an area rife with conflict. If we attack terrorists within these local battles, we must make sure we have the support of the most popular faction behind us. We shouldn't fight against the will of the majority in these situations.

¹⁵You may have to move across marshes.
Move through them quickly without stopping.
You may meet the enemy in the middle of a marsh.
You must keep on the water grasses.
Keep your back to a clump of trees.
This is how you position your army in a marsh.

²¹On a level plateau, take a position that you can change.
Keep the higher ground on your right and to the rear.
Keep danger in front of you and safety behind.
This is how you position yourself on a level plateau.

²⁵You can find an advantage in all four of these situations.
Learn from the great emperor who used positioning to
conquer his four rivals.

Armies are stronger on high ground and weaker on low. 2
They are better camping on sunny southern hillsides than
on shady northern ones.
Provide for your army's health and place men correctly.
Your army will be free from disease.
Done correctly, this means victory.

⁶You must sometimes defend on a hill or riverbank.
You must keep on the south side in the sun.
Keep the uphill slope at your right rear.

⁹This will give the advantage to your army.
It will always give you a position of strength.

Marshes are unstable areas and uncertain periods of time. The transitional period in moving toward freedom in the Middle East is such a marsh. Terrorists are going to fight us in this area, and we must counter them by finding islands of stability that we can count on in the region. We have to protect our backs in these situations. We cannot be tempted into questionable missions.

In broad, stable environments where the terrorists have no particular advantage, we must stand on our principles. We should face the terrorist threat directly and line up our traditional economic and social strengths behind us.

In every situation, we must remember that no matter how difficult and varied the environments in which we must counter terrorism, we can leverage the environment against the terrorists.

2 We cannot be shy about claiming the moral high ground in our battle against terrorism. We are stronger making our ideological commitment to freedom visible rather than being subtle about it. The American people and especially our soldiers must be very clear about what we are fighting for. A clear mission protects us from cynicism and leads directly to our success.

We must sometimes defend our methods as well as our mission, but since our methods are also vastly superior to those of the terrorists, defending them also gives us an advantage.

Standing up for what we believe will always give us an advantage. Our leaders must use our values to give us a position of strength.

Stop the march when the rain swells the river into rapids. 3
You may want to ford the river.
Wait until it subsides.

4All regions can have seasonal mountain streams that can
cut you off.
There are seasonal lakes.
There are seasonal blockages.
There are seasonal jungles.
There are seasonal floods.
There are seasonal fissures.
Get away from all these quickly.
Do not get close to them.
Keep them at a distance.
Maneuver the enemy close to them.
Position yourself facing these dangers.
Push the enemy back into them.

16Danger can hide on your army's flank.
There are reservoirs and lakes.
There are reeds and thickets.
There are mountain woods.
Their dense vegetation provides a hiding place.
You must cautiously search through them.
They can always hide an ambush.

3 When the local climate shifts and conditions in an area become chaotic, we must pause in our battle. We shouldn't try to make progress against terrorism during periods of local upheaval.

The Muslim world is historically fractured and unstable, prone to regular upheavals. The ongoing conflict between Israel and Palestine is the most publicized example of this instability, but it is not the central conflict. The predominant political battle in the Muslim world over the last hundred years has been between two equally fascist philosophies: national socialism and Islamic fundamentalism. Iraq and Syria represented the national socialists, while Afghanistan and Iran represented the Islamic fundamentalists. Since the fall of Saddam in Iraq and the Taliban in Afghanistan, the bankruptcy of both philosophies has been broadly exposed. The terrorists have a side to defend in this ongoing political battle, but America doesn't. We should oppose both these failed forms of government and force the terrorists to defend this historical quagmire.

We must also be careful of the hidden dangers in the region. There are vast reservoirs of ancient religious and cultural hostility. There are divisions among sects, clans, and tribes. There are long-standing alliances and ancient enmities. All of these divisions provide breeding grounds for terrorists. We must learn about and bring all these ancient divisions out into the open. We can cautiously use them to our advantage, but we must always be careful about the fact that terrorists can use them against us.

Sometimes, the enemy is close by but remains calm. 4
Expect to find him in a natural stronghold.
Other times he remains at a distance but provokes battle.
He wants you to attack him.

5He sometimes shifts the position of his camp.
He is looking for an advantageous position.

7The trees in the forest move.
Expect that the enemy is coming.
The tall grasses obstruct your view.
Be suspicious.

11The birds take flight.
Expect that the enemy is hiding.
Animals startle.
Expect an ambush.

15Notice the dust.
It sometimes rises high in a straight line.
Vehicles are coming.
The dust appears low in a wide band.
Foot soldiers are coming.
The dust seems scattered in different areas.
The enemy is collecting firewood.
Any dust is light and settling down.
The enemy is setting up camp.

4 Sun Tzu teaches that we cannot take terrorist statements or actions at face value. The basic principle is that deception is central in any war. To understand terrorists, we have to interpret everything that they say or do to understand their situation.

The increased pressure in the Middle East has forced terrorists to look in Africa and Asia for new bases that they can operate from.

If we see signs of increased political instability in Muslim Africa or Asia, we should suspect that terrorists are likely involved. We must be wary about the growth of secret organizations in any of these countries because they are the source of terrorism.

We can know when the terrorists are planning to surprise us by changes in the behavior of others in these regions. We should be listening for chatter not only among the terrorists but among other Muslims to know when the terrorists are planning an attack.

"Dust" exists because nothing can move without leaving some sign. Everything the terrorists do kicks up dirt, leaving signals that we should learn to interpret. Without knowing directly what terrorists are doing, we can get a general idea of their actions by 1) the amount of evidence of activity we find, 2) the pattern of that evidence, and 3) by its increase or decrease. Currently, only its increase or decrease is clear. Our intelligence networks must continually monitor even the smallest rumors about terrorist activities and their pattern to put together a meaningful picture.

Your enemy speaks humbly while building up forces. 5
He is planning to advance.

³The enemy talks aggressively and pushes as if to advance.
He is planning to retreat.

⁵Small vehicles exit his camp first.
They move the army's flanks.
They are forming a battle line.

⁸Your enemy tries to sue for peace but without offering a
treaty.
He is plotting.

¹⁰Your enemy's men run to leave and yet form ranks.
You should expect action.

¹²Half his army advances and the other half retreats.
He is luring you.

¹⁴Your enemy plans to fight but his men just stand there.
They are starving.

¹⁶Those who draw water drink it first.
They are thirsty.

¹⁸Your enemy sees an advantage but does not advance.
His men are tired.

5 The terrorists acted humbly as they built up their organizations to attack, but under increasing pressure their tactics will change.

As we begin hurting them, they will talk more aggressively, even as they plan to fall back and retreat.

If we keep an eye on local terrorist enclaves, when they are planning a coordinated attack we will spot them as they start moving out toward a central target.

When a terrorist leader such as Osama bin Laden sues for a separate peace without ending the war, like he did in making overtures to Europe, his overtures are part of a larger hidden plot.

When terrorist groups pretend to disband but then try to regroup elsewhere, they still want to fight.

When different groups of terrorists emphasize the disagreements they have with each other, they are trying to trick us.

If a group of terrorists has a target and plan but takes no action, it is because it lacks the resources it needs.

As local commanders start running low on funds, they will spend more of their resources on their own physical needs.

As groups of terrorists become tired of the battle, they won't fight even when they have an easy target.

²⁰Birds gather.
Your enemy has abandoned his camp.

²²Your enemy's soldiers call in the night.
They are afraid.

²⁴Your enemy's army is raucous.
The men do not take their commander seriously.

²⁶Your enemy's banners and flags shift.
Order is breaking down.

²⁸Your enemy's officers are irritable.
They are exhausted.

³⁰Your enemy's men kill their horses for meat.
They are out of provisions.

³²They don't put their pots away or return to their tents.
They are desperate.

³⁴Enemy troops appear sincere and agreeable.
But their men are slow to speak to each other.
They are no longer united.

³⁷Your enemy offers too many incentives to his men.
He is in trouble.

³⁹Your enemy gives out too many punishments.
His men are weary.

As terrorist groups abandon their camps, other local people will come to pick through their leavings.

As terrorists grow more frightened about the way the war is going, we will hear more and more complaints through the media.

As terrorists start to lose confidence in their leaders, they will become more and more undisciplined and erratic.

As trust within the terrorist community begins to break down, various factions will align themselves.

As we increase the pressure on them, the most dedicated terrorists will grow increasingly angry.

As they run out of resources, terrorists and ex-terrorists will start selling whatever they have to feed themselves.

When they become truly desperate, they will abandon their belongings and leave their organizations.

As the various sects within terrorism become more divided, they will still pretend that they are working together, but they will communicate less and less often.

We motivate individuals to join us out of self-interest, but if we have to bribe them, they don't see the real benefit of the alliance.

When members of terrorist organizations start to give up, their leaders will turn on them.

⁴¹Your enemy first acts violently and then is afraid of your
larger force.
His best troops have not arrived.

⁴³Your enemy comes in a conciliatory manner.
He needs to rest and recuperate.

⁴⁵Your enemy is angry and appears to welcome battle.
This goes on for a long time, but he doesn't attack.
He also doesn't leave the field.
You must watch him carefully.

If you are too weak to fight, you must find more men. 6
In this situation, you must not act aggressively.
You must unite your forces.
Prepare for the enemy.
Recruit men and stay where you are.

⁶You must be cautious about making plans and adjust to the
enemy.
You must gather more men.

When we meet poorly trained and less dedicated groups of terrorists, they will first act like they want to fight but then they will quickly run away from battle.

When they need to rest and recuperate, groups that have supported the terrorists will try to make peace with us.

When they are really beaten, terrorists will still make a big show and claim that they still want to fight with us, but they won't launch any more attacks. However, they still won't surrender. We will always have to keep a close eye on them.

6 When the terrorists become too weak to fight, they will go back to trying to grow their organizations. They will stop launching aggressive attacks, but they will focus on bringing all their supporters back together. They will go back to preparing for battle, recruiting their men, and hiding among their supporters.

They will become more cautious about the plans they make. They will try to adjust their strategy to their new position. They will have to rebuild their organizations to continue their war.

With new, undedicated soldiers, you can depend on them 7
if you discipline them.
They will tend to disobey your orders.
If they do not obey your orders, they will be useless.

4You can depend on seasoned, dedicated soldiers.
But you must avoid disciplining them without reason.
Otherwise, you cannot use them.

7You must control your soldiers with esprit de corps.
You must bring them together by winning victories.
You must get them to believe in you.

10Make it easy for people to know what to do by training
your people.
Your people will then obey you.
If you do not make it easy for people to know what to do,
you won't train your people.
Then they will not obey.

14Make your commands easy to follow.
You must understand the way a crowd thinks.

7 As Muslim nations rebuild in the aftermath of the collapse of national socialism and Islamic fundamentalism, the new, undedicated citizens in these societies will require discipline. They will tend to ignore laws, and if the laws are not enforced, these nations will fail.

The nations will have to depend on the most dedicated and productive members of society, but we must avoid over-regulating them without reason. Productive people are what we need.

The secret to winning this war is creating a sense of direction and purpose in Muslim society. The people must see that they can be successful. They must have confidence that they can build a future.

America can make this easy by training people to do productive work. If people have a career, they will have direction in their lives. They will then obey the laws of society. If people do not know how to make a living, they cannot support themselves in a productive way and cannot be controlled. They will try to make a living by breaking the laws.

America must make it easy for Muslims in these regions to obey the law. We must understand their local psychology.

Chapter 10

地 形

Field Position: Evaluating Our Options

This chapter examines six characteristics that strategists use to evaluate their options. In this case, we use these characteristics to evaluate our real choices in the War on Terror. Sun Tzu teaches that success in war is a matter of using each successive field position to move progressively toward our long-term goal. Each field position is evaluated based on its potential to help us move forward or defend ourselves. Each field position acts as a stepping-stone to a future position, but to use a field position correctly we must understand how its characteristics affect us.

In the conflict so far, both we and the terrorists have shown that we have weaknesses. America has been under direct attack by Islamic fundamentalism for decades, but our initial responses were tepid and uncertain. Even now, we still show limited skill in fighting the larger media war that is the real basis for terror. However, the terrorists have shown more serious weaknesses, especially since we have taken the war to their home territory.

Strategy depends on knowledge. Both our leaders and the American public must know more about Islamic history and philosophy in order to fight this war. The better educated we are, the more we will pressure the media into discussing the real historical and philosophical issues at stake. Only that discussion will force the media to throw away the David-versus-Goliath script that it has been using thus far in describing this conflict. To win the media war, we don't need less reporting but more reporting.

Field Position

SUN TZU SAID:

Some field positions are unobstructed. 1
Some field positions are entangling.
Some field positions are supporting.
Some field positions are constricted.
Some field positions give you a barricade.
Some field positions are spread out.

7You can attack from some positions easily.
Other forces can meet you easily as well.
We call these unobstructed positions.
These positions are open.
In them, be the first to occupy a high, sunny area.
Put yourself where you can defend your supply routes.
Then you will have an advantage.

Evaluating Our Options

1 We must evaluate our real options in the War on Terror. Sun Tzu defines these options by six extremes. Some of our options leave us open to move or to be attacked. Others entangle us, making retreat impossible. Other options support us, making movement undesirable. Some options wall us in and the terrorists out. Some options spread our resources too thinly.

When we moved into Iraq and Afghanistan, we moved into *open* field positions. We can attack terrorist strongholds more easily from these positions, but terrorists can also attack us more easily as well. Like all our real-world options, our open positions in the Middle East are neither good nor bad in themselves. Their value comes from how we use them. These positions are very powerful as long as we control them and aren't cut off in them.

14You can attack from some positions easily.

Disaster arises when you try to return to them.

These are entangling positions.

These field positions are one-sided.

Wait until your enemy is unprepared.

You can then attack from these positions and win.

Avoid a well-prepared enemy.

You will try to attack and lose.

Since you can't return, you will meet disaster.

These field positions offer no advantage.

24You cannot leave some positions without losing an advantage.

If the enemy leaves this ground, he also loses an advantage.

We call these supporting field positions.

These positions strengthen you.

The enemy may try to entice you away.

Still, hold your position.

You must entice the enemy to leave.

You then strike him as he is leaving.

These field positions offer an advantage.

33Some field positions are constricted.

Get to these positions first.

You must fill these areas and await the enemy.

Sometimes, the enemy will reach them first.

If he fills them, do not follow him.

However, if he fails to fill them, you can go after him.

We know that our positions in the Middle East are entangling. However, Sun Tzu teaches that the problem with entangling positions is not that you can't leave them, but that if you do leave them, you can never return. Saudi Arabia was an entangling position. We moved out of Saudi Arabia to move into Iraq, knowing that we could not return to our bases there. We could theoretically abandon Iraq and Afghanistan today if we wanted to, but if we did we would never have any credibility in those countries again. If we do move forward from these positions in the War on Terror, we must make sure that our new positions are stronger.

We get stuck in entangling positions because we can't return, but we get stuck in supporting positions because the opportunities that they offer are so good that we cannot abandon them. Supporting positions are positions that we should make long-term commitments to holding. Iraq, because of its central location in the Middle East, may be an ideal supporting position in the area. No matter what happens longer term within the Iraqi government, we will want bases in Iraq to protect our vital interests in the region. Those who want to abandon Iraq have no appreciation for its unique strategic position.

Constricted positions are the opposite of spread-out positions. They are good defensive positions, locking up key locations to prevent an opponent's attack. The Golan Heights are a good example. They were the key in Israel's defense against Syria in both 1967 and 1973 when Syrian forces failed to fill them. Israel has occupied them since 1973 because of their strategic importance to defense.

39Some field positions give you a barricade.
Get to these positions first.
You must occupy their southern, sunny heights in order to
await the enemy.
Sometimes the enemy occupies these areas first.
If so, entice him away.
Never go after him.

45Some field positions are too spread out.
Your force may seem equal to the enemy.
Still you will lose if you provoke a battle.
If you fight, you will not have any advantage.

49These are the six types of field positions.
Each battleground has its own rules.
As a commander, you must know where to go.
You must examine each position closely.

Some armies can be outmaneuvered. 2
Some armies are too lax.
Some armies fall down.
Some armies fall apart.
Some armies are disorganized.
Some armies must retreat.

7Know all six of these weaknesses.
They create weak timing and disastrous positions.
They all arise from the army's commander.

Barricaded positions are the opposite of open positions. A barricaded position is meant to prevent attacks, but in doing so, it also eliminates our ability to attack. Those who suggest that America should withdraw its military forces to within its borders are suggesting a barricaded position. North Korea is an example of an enemy in the War on Terror that has a successful barricaded position. We cannot attack it directly because doing so is too dangerous.

We cannot have our troops everywhere. Spreading our forces weakens our position. Though we can threaten Syria and Iran from Iraq, we cannot attack both countries at once or at all until we are ready to move our troops into those new positions.

Each position is ideally a stepping-stone to a better position. Each opens up new opportunities and poses new dangers. As we move forward in the War on Terror, we must consider each step carefully and know precisely what we are trying to accomplish.

2 In fighting terror, we must make certain that our own forces have none of these weaknesses while spotting these weaknesses in terrorist organizations. Thus far, we have managed to outmaneuver the terrorists by moving into the Middle East. Their armies have either fallen apart, been disorganized, or had to retreat. However, we must be wary of our weaknesses on the media battleground.

We must be aware of our potential vulnerabilities in the media battle. Our political and military leaders must be as skilled at communication strategy as they are at military strategy.

10One general can command a force equal to the enemy.
Still his enemy outflanks him.
This means that his army can be outmaneuvered.

13Another can have strong soldiers but weak officers.
This means that his army is too lax.

15Another has strong officers but weak soldiers.
This means that his army will fall down.

17Another has subcommanders that are angry and defiant.
They attack the enemy and fight their own battles.
The commander cannot know the battlefield.
This means that his army will fall apart.

21Another general is weak and easygoing.
He fails to make his orders clear.
His officers and men lack direction.
This shows in his military formations.
This means that his army is disorganized.

26Another general fails to predict the enemy.
He pits his small forces against larger ones.
His weak forces attack stronger ones.
He fails to pick his fights correctly.
This means that his army must retreat.

Though our leaders have complete access to the media, they have often been outmaneuvered by the terrorists, who know how to grab the headlines and push the emotional buttons of the press.

Often our soldiers have better stories for the media than their officers do. Our officers are too relaxed in fighting the media war.

Terrorist leaders, in contrast, make strong threats, but they can seldom back them up, so their credibility suffers.

A flaw in the network of terror is that terrorist groups are fragmented. They vent their frustration at military setbacks at the hands of America by attacking fellow Muslims in countries such as Saudi Arabia. This reaction undermines support for their cause.

Before 9/11, America's leadership was weak and too accepting of attacks on our people. Our military response to repeated terrorist attacks was indifferent. Because we weren't trying to establish clear positions, we couldn't make any progress against the terrorists. Our efforts were halfhearted and disorganized.

Since 9/11, the terrorists and their supporters have miscalculated America's resolve. They have found themselves fighting superior forces over and over again. In the initial battles for Afghanistan and Iraq and in the resistance since, our opponents have had to retreat every time they tried to stand against us.

³¹You must know all about these six weaknesses.
You must understand the philosophies that lead to defeat.
When a general arrives, you can know what he will do.
You must study each general carefully.

You must control your field position. 3
It will always strengthen your army.

³You must predict the enemy to overpower him and win.
You must analyze the obstacles, dangers, and distances.
This is the best way to command.

⁶Understand your field position before you go to battle.
Then you will win.
You can fail to understand your field position and meet
opponents.
Then you will fail.

¹⁰You must provoke battle when you will certainly win.
It doesn't matter what you are ordered.
The government may order you not to fight.
Despite that, you must always fight when you will win.

¹⁴Sometimes provoking a battle will lead to a loss.
The government may order you to fight.
Despite that, you must avoid battle when you will lose.

Will the terrorists keep making the same mistakes? Will we return to the mistakes we have made in the past? It all depends on our respective leaders. As American and terrorist leadership evolves, we must pay attention to the mistakes these leaders are prone to make.

3 Success in the War on Terror comes from making the right decisions about where and when to move forward.

We can predict that terrorists will try to use their mobility to make quick, dramatic strikes. We and our allies must create obstacles to their easy movement in order to slow them down.

We must lure the terrorists into fixed positions in havens such as Syria and Iran where they feel safe. We can then attack them at will. As long as we force the terrorists to move around, we cannot know where they are located. This prevents us from attacking. Fighting terrorism requires control of their positions.

When the time is right, we can provoke a battle with the terrorists in Syria and Iran. It doesn't matter if the UN and others oppose it. Many leaders throughout the world oppose a strong American military. Despite that fact, we must fight battles we can win.

When we do not have solid terrorist targets, we must avoid confrontations. Even if public opinion wants us to take action, we must avoid action when we have no opportunity to win.

[17]You must advance without desiring praise.
You must retreat without fearing shame.
The only correct move is to preserve your troops.
This is how you serve your country.
This is how you reward your nation.

Think of your soldiers as little children. 4
You can make them follow you into a deep river.
Treat them as your beloved children.
You can lead them all to their deaths.

[5]Some leaders are generous but cannot use their men.
They love their men but cannot command them.
Their men are unruly and disorganized.
These leaders create spoiled children.
Their soldiers are useless.

You may know what your soldiers will do in an attack. 5
You may not know if the enemy is vulnerable to attack.
You will then win only half the time.
You may know that the enemy is vulnerable to attack.
You may not know if your men have the capability of attack-
ing him.
You will still win only half the time.
You may know that the enemy is vulnerable to attack.
You may know that your men are ready to attack.
You may not, however, know how to position yourself in the
field for battle.
You will still win only half the time.

Our leaders must not make war out of personal pride. They must also be free to retreat when necessary without embarrassment. We must always have leaders who are concerned about the lives of our fighting men. Our leaders must be trusted to act in the nation's best interests. This is how we keep America successful.

4 Sun Tzu teaches that leaders must care deeply about those who serve in the military. This is one big difference between America and the terrorists. Terrorists don't care about preserving the lives of their soldiers. Americans care deeply about our soldiers' safety.

However, to protect our soldiers, we must be careful to maintain military discipline. We saw at Abu Ghraib prison how badly undisciplined soldiers can hurt us. We are still having serious problems with the new co-ed military and sexual activity within the ranks. This lack of discipline can endanger lives.

5 If we move against Syria or Iran, we can know what our military will do in the attack, but those attacks are dangerous because we cannot yet be certain of how the Syrians or Iranians will respond.

On the media front, especially in the Arab world, we know that terrorists should be attacked as savages, but we do not yet have the credibility to pose that attack successfully. This means that we lose these battles as often as we win them.

To be able to advance either on the ground or in the media, we must know that the terrorists are vulnerable to attack, and we must know how to attack them. We must also know how to use our military position and our media image to reinforce one another. If we are not consistent, we will lose one battle or the other.

[11]You must know how to make war.
You can then act without confusion.
You can attempt anything.

[14]We say:
Know the enemy and know yourself.
Your victory will be painless.
Know the weather and the field.
Your victory will be complete.

♦ ♦ ♦

We must have clear goals on the ground and in the media. Then all our people can act without confusion. As we meet our goals, the terrorists will come to believe we can do anything.

The secret to winning the War on Terror is understanding the true nature of the terrorists' threat and our true character. With that deep understanding we can win this war easily. However, if we want to win this war completely, we must control the battlegrounds and leverage the climate of the times.

♦ ♦ ♦

Chapter 11

九地

Types of Terrain: Responding to Terror

The term "terrain" used in this title also means "situation." This chapter describes nine situations that arise during a campaign in any war. To initially illustrate these situations, we will describe how they unfolded during the American invasion of Iraq, but this is the most simplistic view of these situations. On a deeper level, each of these situations represents a special form of strategic challenge. We will see variations of these challenges elsewhere in the world in other battles in the War on Terror.

This chapter, like much of this book, is a history of what has happened thus far, a prediction of what will happen in the future, and a prescription for how we should react in these common situations. Sometimes American forces will find themselves in these situations, and our leaders must respond appropriately. Other times, the terrorists will find themselves in these situations, and our leaders must know how to counter their responses. Unfortunately, the media does not understand these situations and almost always misreports why our military reacts the way it does.

We describe these nine situations as stages in a military campaign because Sun Tzu presents them in the order that they tend to occur. The first stages arise early in a military campaign. These early stages lead to more complicated and difficult stages. This progression ends with the most dangerous and delicate stages. We have already seen all of these stages at least once in our War on Terror, and we will see them again.

Types of Terrain

SUN TZU SAID:

Use the art of war. 1
Know when the terrain will scatter you.
Know when the terrain is easy.
Know when the terrain is disputed.
Know when the terrain is open.
Know when the terrain is intersecting.
Know when the terrain is dangerous.
Know when the terrain is bad.
Know when the terrain is confined.
Know when the terrain is deadly.

[11]Warring parties must sometimes fight inside their own
territory.
This is scattering terrain.

[13]When you enter hostile territory, your penetration is shallow.
This is easy terrain.

[15]Some terrain gives you an advantageous position.
But it gives others an advantageous position as well.
This is disputed terrain.

Responding to Terror

1 Good strategy demands knowing the proper response to the different situations that will arise in the War on Terror. The first of the nine common situations divides our forces, scattering us. The second situation allows for easy progress. The third situation creates conflict. The fourth situation is like a race. The fifth situation brings together different groups to a rallying point. In the sixth situation, a deep invasion becomes dangerous. The seventh situation arises when inevitable difficulties must be struggled through. The eighth situation arises when forces are surrounded. The final situation arises in battles to the death.

The battles over terrorism within our own borders tend to divide us. Though we were not invaded on 9/11, even discussion about the terrorist threat accentuates our political divisions.

We made limited investments in winning the battle for Afghanistan. This made it easy ground.

The oil riches of the Middle East make the area important for the whole world. This ensures that different nations—such as France and America—will have conflicting interests there.

[18]You can use some terrain to advance easily.
Others can advance along with you.
This is open terrain.

[21]Everyone shares access to a given area.
The first one to arrive there can gather a larger group than
anyone else.
This is intersecting terrain.

[24]You can penetrate deeply into hostile territory.
Then many hostile cities are behind you.
This is dangerous terrain.

[27]There are mountain forests.
There are dangerous obstructions.
There are reservoirs.
Everyone confronts these obstacles on a campaign.
They make bad terrain.

[32]In some areas, the entry passage is narrow.
You are closed in as you try to get out of them.
In this type of area, a few people can effectively attack your
much larger force.
This is confined terrain.

[36]You can sometimes survive only if you fight quickly.
You will die if you delay.
This is deadly terrain.

During the 1980s, when America was focused on fighting communism, the situation was open. America and the terrorists were both able to advance their respective causes without direct conflict.

When many nations' interests come together, we have an intersecting situation. This is what makes the situation in North Korea so different from the situation in Iraq under Saddam. China, South Korea, Japan, and even Russia are involved in North Korea.

Our heavy investment of money and people made the war in Iraq much more dangerous than the war in Afghanistan. It left us exposed to enemy attacks on our ability to support our soldiers.

This situation explains the problem in finding Osama bin Laden. The region between Afghanistan and Pakistan is typical bad terrain. The region is so difficult that bin Laden may well be dead, but we will never know it. All we can do in this situation is keep going, trying to find and kill him.

Confined terrain describes narrow passages or transition points where larger forces are sensitive to attack by smaller groups. The turnover of sovereignty to Iraq was such a transition, and America made a huge mistake by announcing the date, but we recovered by surprising the terrorists by making the turnover two days early.

This is the situation we face when we think terrorists might get weapons of mass destruction. We must act immediately to stop them because too many people will die if we delay.

³⁹To be successful, you must control scattering terrain by
avoiding battle.

Control easy terrain by not stopping.

Control disputed terrain by not attacking.

Control open terrain by staying with the enemy's forces.

Control intersecting terrain by uniting with your allies.

Control dangerous terrain by plundering.

Control bad terrain by keeping on the move.

Control confined terrain by using surprise.

Control deadly terrain by fighting.

Go to an area that is known to be good for waging war. **2**
Use it to cut off the enemy's contact between his front and
back lines.

Prevent his small parties from relying on his larger force.

Stop his strong divisions from rescuing his weak ones.

Prevent his officers from getting their men together.

Chase his soldiers apart to stop them from amassing.

Harass them to prevent their ranks from forming.

⁸When joining battle gives you an advantage, you must do it.

When it isn't to your benefit, you must avoid it.

¹⁰A daring soldier may ask:

"A large, organized enemy army and its general are coming.
What do I do to prepare for them?"

We went to war in the Middle East to avoid fighting terrorists within our borders. After the easy war in Afghanistan, we made the right decision by not stopping. We must avoid battles over the oil wealth of the region. During the eighties and later in the nineties, we fell behind the terrorists by not responding to them. To deal with North Korea, we must work with our allies. During the dangerous Iraq war, our inability to use Iraq's riches forced us to raise more money from taxpayers. All we can do to find bin Laden is keep looking. We must keep future transition points a secret to save lives. We cannot hesitate to kill terrorists when lives are threatened.

2 We made war in the Middle East because it was a good battleground for our forces. We used this war to drive a physical wedge between the nations that support terror. This prevents the relatively small terrorist groups from relying on at least two of the major states that previously supported terror. These wars cut the lines of communication between Al Qaeda's leaders and its followers. These wars fragmented terrorism; pitting the terrorists against governments that once tolerated them in Saudi Arabia, Turkey, and Pakistan.

We had to invade the Middle East to create a strong position at the source of terror. We must avoid fighting the terrorists here in America.

Fear is the weapon of terror. We are right to ask, "What happens if the terrorists get organized behind a strong leader and come after us here? How can we prepare for them?"

[13]Tell him:
"First seize an area that the enemy must have.
Then he will pay attention to you.
Mastering speed is the essence of war.
Take advantage of a large enemy's inability to keep up.
Use a philosophy of avoiding difficult situations.
Attack the area where he doesn't expect you."

You must use the philosophy of an invader. 3
Invade deeply and then concentrate your forces.
This controls your men without oppressing them.

[4]Get your supplies from the riches of the territory.
They are sufficient to supply your whole army.

[6]Take care of your men and do not overtax them.
Your esprit de corps increases your momentum.
Keep your army moving and plan for surprises.
Make it difficult for the enemy to count your forces.
Position your men where there is no place to run.
They will then face death without fleeing.
They will find a way to survive.
Your officers and men will fight to their utmost.

[14]Military officers who are committed lose their fear.
When they have nowhere to run, they must stand firm.
Deep in enemy territory, they are captives.
Since they cannot escape, they will fight.

The only way to prevent terrorists from attacking us here is to keep the battle in the Middle East. Our invasion there forces the terrorists to respond on their home ground, and this exaggerates the divisions within their movement. For almost twenty-five years, we were slow to react to terrorist attacks, so they kept escalating. After 9/11, we responded quickly, attacking Afghanistan within weeks, and the terrorists have been fighting defensive actions ever since then.

3 Our philosophy of invasion brought the war to the Middle East. Muslims must now concentrate on defending themselves against terrorists. They have become our allies without our forcing them.

Resources from Saudi Arabia, Turkey, and Pakistan are now overtly fighting terrorism where they once covertly supported it.

We can support these nations without alienating their people. Our success in defeating terrorists will increase the Muslim appetite for fighting terrorism. As the war progresses, Muslims will be better prepared for terrorist attacks. Terrorists will get less and less support. We have forced Muslims to stand against their fanatics. These Muslims will not back down as terrorists try to kill them. They will fight fanatics as they have throughout history. Their leaders and people will fight with all their resources.

Once people are committed to the battle, terrorists lose their ability to intimidate. Muslims won't be able to blame America or Israel for terrorism and will stand firm against it. Muslims must see that they are trapped by terrorism and that they must fight it.

¹⁸Commit your men completely.
Without being posted, they will be on guard.
Without being asked, they will get what is needed.
Without being forced, they will be dedicated.
Without being given orders, they can be trusted.

²³Stop them from guessing by removing all their doubts.
Stop them from dying by giving them no place to run.

²⁵Your officers may not be rich.
Nevertheless, they still desire plunder.
They may die young.
Nevertheless, they still want to live forever.

²⁹You must order the time of attack.
Officers and men may sit and weep until their lapels are wet.
When they stand up, tears may stream down their cheeks.
Put them in a position where they cannot run.
They will show the greatest courage under fire.

Make good use of war. 4
This demands instant reflexes.
You must develop these instant reflexes.
Act like an ordinary mountain snake.
If people strike your head then stop them with your tail.
If they strike your tail then stop them with your head.
If they strike your middle then use both your head and tail.

The Muslim people must know that their future depends totally on their own commitment. Then they will be on guard for the terrorists without being ordered. They will take the initiative to do what is needed to pacify their nation. Though not dedicated to freedom, they are dedicated to serving their own well-being.

The terrorists have made it clear that this is a battle to the death. When others realize that they are at risk, they will defend themselves.

Most Muslims might be poor, but nevertheless they still want the economic freedom to become financially successful. Life might be cheap in the Islamic world, but individual Muslims still want to survive and have their children survive.

Muslims throughout the world have no choice in this battle. Their leaders will still complain about America and the Jews. Even when they are forced to defend themselves, they will continue to blame us. But as long as they don't have any other choice, they will stand firm and find the courage to stop the terrorists among them.

4 The Muslim people must join the War on Terror. They must work together to strike back instantly when terrorists attack. They must develop automatic responses. The whole region must become a dangerous place for terrorists. If terrorists attack Muslim leaders, the people must rise to their nation's defense. If terrorists strike at innocent civilians, Muslim nations must strike back immediately. If terrorists strike any Islamic nation, all Islamic nations must respond.

⁸A daring soldier asks:
"Can any army imitate these instant reflexes?"
We answer:
"It can."

¹²To command and get the most out of proud people, you
must study adversity.
People work together when they are in the same boat during
a storm.
In this situation, one rescues the other just as the right
hand helps the left.

¹⁵Use adversity correctly.
Tether your horses and bury your wagon's wheels.
Still, you can't depend on this alone.
An organized force is braver than lone individuals.
This is the art of organization.
Put the tough and weak together.
You must also use the terrain.

²²Make good use of war.
Unite your men as one.
Never let them give up.

The commander must be a military professional. 5
This requires confidence and detachment.
You must maintain dignity and order.
You must control what your men see and hear.
They must follow you without knowing your plans.

Can the countries in a divided region develop the ability to act quickly in response to terrorist attacks? They can if they must. Until they learn to respond quickly, they will all remain a target for terrorism and they will be mired in an ongoing struggle.

To bring Muslims together, we must help them see that terrorism is a threat to them all. The many different groups and tribes within the area must realize that their fate is intertwined in the coming struggle. Shiites, Sunnis, and all other sects, tribes, and nationalities must work together in order to protect themselves. Historically, Muslims come together when they are threatened.

We must use the difficulties in the region to unite Muslims against terror. Muslims cannot run from the terrorist threat, but this alone doesn't guarantee that they will work together. We must encourage an Islamic alliance so that each nation doesn't become a haven for terrorists from other nations. In this organization, the stronger nations must support the weaker nations. We must use our presence in the region to encourage this organization.

We must make good use of the war. We must unite into our coalition everyone who is willing to fight terror. We must threaten any nation that tolerates terrorists.

5 As head of a coalition against terror that represents more than a billion people, America must act responsibly. We can be both confident and objective. We must insist on order and respect. We must show the world what terrorism does and what it stands for. We must have people trust us without having to defend our plans.

⁶You can reinvent your men's roles.

You can change your plans.

You can use your men without their understanding.

⁹You must shift your campgrounds.

You must take detours from the ordinary routes.

You must use your men without giving them your strategy.

¹²A commander provides what is needed now.

This is like climbing high and being willing to kick away your ladder.

You must be able to lead your men deep into different surrounding territory.

And yet, you can discover the opportunity to win.

¹⁶You must drive men like a flock of sheep.

You must drive them to march.

You must drive them to attack.

You must never let them know where you are headed.

You must unite them into a great army.

You must then drive them against all opposition.

This is the job of a true commander.

²³You must adapt to the different terrain.

You must adapt to find an advantage.

You must manage your people's affections.

You must study all these skills.

America can change the role it plays in the War on Terror. When we need to, we can change our plans and commitments. We can use partnerships without giving the terrorists weapon against us.

To protect key people against assassination, we must not keep them in fixed locations. Key people must change their travel plans and routes. They must learn to keep their travel plans a secret.

We should give our partners only what they need to address their immediate needs. We must get other nations heavily invested in fighting terror but let them fight on their own. We must lead other nations into this war by forcing them to choose sides. We cannot be shy about forcing other nations to take sides. This is the only way we can find an opportunity to win.

We cannot afford to be easy on other nations in our battle against terror. We must push them to move. We must force them to attack and defeat the terrorists among them. We need America to be dangerous and unpredictable. We must get commitments, especially from Muslim nations, to unite with us against terror. We must make them take sides against the terrorists. This responsibility falls to America as the nation leading the fight against terror.

We must adapt to the changing situation throughout the world. We must change our diplomatic policies to enlist support against terror. We must do a better job managing how people feel about America. We must use our skill at marketing.

Always use the philosophy of invasion. 6
Deep invasions concentrate your forces.
Shallow invasions scatter your forces.
When you leave your country and cross the border, you must
take control.
This is always critical ground.
You can sometimes move in any direction.
This is always intersecting ground.
You can penetrate deeply into a territory.
This is always dangerous ground.
You penetrate only a little way.
This is always easy ground.
Your retreat is closed and the path ahead tight.
This is always confined ground.
There is sometimes no place to run.
This is always deadly ground.

[16]To use scattering terrain correctly, you must inspire your
men's devotion.
On easy terrain, you must keep in close communication.
On disputed terrain, you try to hamper the enemy's progress.
On open terrain, you must carefully defend your chosen position.
On intersecting terrain, you must solidify your alliances.
On dangerous terrain, you must ensure your food supplies.
On bad terrain, you must keep advancing along the road.
On confined terrain, you must stop information leaks from
your headquarters.
On deadly terrain, you must show what you can do by
killing the enemy.

6 We must maintain our initiative as an invader in this war. Our deep commitment to the War on Terror focuses our efforts. If we let ourselves get attacked again, we must protect ourselves against internal political divisions.

When we mobilize our forces to attack another country, we must be certain we can afford the invasion. These invasions are as dangerous as they are necessary. This is why we avoid invasions when we have other options, as in North Korea. The larger the country and the more troops we have to involve, the more dangerous invasion becomes.

If we can work with internal opposition to overthrow the governments in Syria or Iran as we did in Afghanistan, we will use our forces more sparingly. These battles are much easier and less expensive to win. During delicate transitions, we must be more careful about announcing our timing. In this war, we cannot make peace with the terrorists. We must kill them before they kill us.

To protect ourselves from political divisions caused by future attacks, our leaders must call for us to unite in patriotism. We must be in contact with insurgents in Syria and Iran. We must prevent terrorists from getting support from the wealth of Middle Eastern oil. We must not leave openings for future opponents as we did for Islamic terrorists. We must use our allies to control North Korea. We must make sure that we can afford future invasions into Syria or Iran if they become necessary. We cannot become discouraged in searching for bin Laden. During sensitive transitions, we must stop the information leaks coming from within our government. In the end, we must realize that this is a war to the death. It is not a legal action. We must be willing to kill terrorists before the kill us.

²⁵Make your men feel like an army.
Surround them and they will defend themselves.
If they cannot avoid it, they will fight.
If they are under pressure, they will obey.

Do the right thing when you don't know your 7
different enemies' plans.
Don't attempt to meet them.

³You don't know the position of mountain forests, dangerous
obstructions, and reservoirs?
Then you cannot march the army.
You don't have local guides?
You won't get any of the benefits of the terrain.

⁷There are many factors in war.
You may lack knowledge of any one of them.
If so, it is wrong to take a nation into war.

¹⁰You must be able to control your government's war.
If you divide a big nation, it will be unable to put together a
large force.
Increase your enemy's fear of your ability.
Prevent his forces from getting together and organizing.

People all over the world must identify with their defenders. We must all realize that we are surrounded and that we must defend ourselves. We cannot avoid this fight, so we must commit ourselves to it. The danger from terrorists must unite us, not divide us.

7 As long as we do not know who supports terrorists and who is against them, we must be careful. We shouldn't commit to supporting any group unless we know exactly where it stands.

We must know specifically which individuals, groups, and foreign interests are working to obstruct the War on Terror. Without this knowledge, we cannot move forward. Unless we are getting good information from those knowledgeable in local politics, we will not be able to build on our position in the Middle East.

There are many different things that will affect the War on Terror. We need good intelligence in every area in order to survive. Without good information, we cannot win this war.

We must choose the right politicians for fighting the war. If politics divide our nation, we will be unable to fight any major battles in the future. Our ability to fight these battles is what discourages nations such as Syria and Iran from supporting terrorists. If these nations are not afraid of us, terrorists will organize within them.

¹⁴Do the right thing and do not arrange outside alliances
before their time.
You will not have to assert your authority prematurely.
Trust only yourself and your self-interest.
This increases the enemy's fear of you.
You can make one of his allies withdraw.
His whole nation can fall.

²⁰Distribute rewards without worrying about having a system.
Halt without the government's command.
Attack with the whole strength of your army.
Use your army as if it were a single man.

²⁴Attack with skill.
Do not discuss it.
Attack when you have an advantage.
Do not talk about the dangers.
When you can launch your army into deadly ground, even if
it stumbles, it can still survive.
You can be weakened in a deadly battle and yet be stronger
afterward.

³⁰Even a large force can fall into misfortune.
If you fall behind, however, you can still turn defeat into victory.
You must use the skills of war.
To survive, you must adapt yourself to your enemy's purpose.
You must stay with him no matter where he goes.
It may take a thousand miles to kill the general.
If you correctly understand him, you can find the skill to do it.

We shouldn't get the UN, NATO, or other outside governments involved in any future battle prematurely. If we do, our decisions and authority to act are likely to be challenged. We must be guided only by our own best interests. Our ability to act unilaterally is what the terrorists are really afraid of. They are concerned that their own allies could start to turn on them. If we can get their Muslim supporters to abandon them, they will fail.

America must become better at articulating how fighting terror rewards everyone. We must be able to disengage our military without getting approval from other nations. When we move against terrorists, we must use all our resources. We must be united.

If we need to move against terrorists in Syria, Iran, or elsewhere, we must do it skillfully. We must not open the issue to world discussion. We must move when we see a clear advantage in moving. We cannot worry about the risks. If we continually work to improve our position, we are bound to make some mistakes, but our nation will be more certain to survive. These deadly battles are costly in lives and money, so we must choose only battles that make America stronger over time.

America is powerful, but we will not always be lucky. We could suffer another successful terrorist attack, but it must spur us to greater success. We must use all our technology and science. To survive, we must learn to think like the terrorists instead of pretending that they think like we do. We must keep pressuring the terrorists wherever they seek refuge. We go anywhere to kill the terrorists' leaders. If we understand their thinking, we can do it.

Manage your government correctly at the start of a war. 8
Close your borders and tear up passports.
Block the passage of envoys.
Encourage the halls of power to rise to the occasion.
You must use any means to put an end to politics.
Your enemy's people will leave you an opening.
You must instantly invade through it.

[8]Immediately seize a place that they love.
Do it quickly.
Trample any border to pursue the enemy.
Use your judgment about when to fight.

[12]Doing the right thing at the start of war is like
approaching a woman.
Your enemy's men must open the door.
After that, you should act like a streaking rabbit.
The enemy will be unable to catch you.

✦ ✦ ✦

Meanwhile, we must be diligent on the home front. We must tighten up our borders. We must get better control over who can come here. We must keep out the terrorists' sympathizers. We must keep politicians from hampering the defense of the country. National defense cannot be undermined by international politics. Eventually, the terrorists will give us another opportunity to strike them. We cannot let international politics slow down our response.

If the terrorists attack us again, we should immediately go after their supporters in Syria, Iran, or even France. We must act instantly. We must ignore international borders to go after our enemies. We must attack targets that we identify as dangerous.

We must be passionate in seeking to advance our position in the War on Terror. The terrorists or their supporters must give us an opening, but when they do we cannot hesitate. We must act so quickly that we catch everyone by surprise. Our opponents in the world cannot stop us.

♦ ♦ ♦

Chapter 12

Attacking with Fire: Fighting the Message War

Although Sun Tzu uses this chapter to cover a specific weapon, fire, its broader topic is leveraging forces in the environment as weapons. In our battle with terrorists, the critical environmental weapon is the communication industry that distributes information as entertainment and shapes this war.

We began this book by saying that terrorism was made possible by changes in the media. Islamic fundamentalists discovered that the media could be manipulated by acts of terror to publicize their cause, generating donations and support. In response, we use the media to undermine this strategy.

Though America is cast as the evil giant in this battle, our best weapon is the truth. The truth is that terrorism is a corrupt and destructive force. Terrorists make better villains than victims. We only need to put human faces on the innocent people they behead, blow up, intimidate, and use as human shields.

To use the media as a weapon, America must change its approach to information. Our repugnance for propaganda, our concern for legalities, and our need for secrecy have prevented us from working well with the press. In making the terrorists into the villains, telling the truth is not propaganda. We are fighting a war, not building a legal case. While we don't want the government controlling the media, we can certainly be more intelligent about helping the media cast the terrorists as villains in this story. This message is timely, interesting, and true.

Attacking with Fire

SUN TZU SAID:

There are five ways of attacking with fire. 1
The first is burning troops.
The second is burning supplies.
The third is burning supply transport.
The fourth is burning storehouses.
The fifth is burning camps.

7To make fire, you must have the resources.
To build a fire, you must prepare the raw materials.

9To attack with fire, you must be in the right season.
To start a fire, you must have the time.

11Choose the right season.
The weather must be dry.

13Choose the right time.
Pick a season when the grass is as high as the side of a cart.

15You can tell the proper days by the stars in the night sky.
You want days when the wind rises in the morning.

Fighting the Message War

1 America must have a message which targets the terrorists'
resources. We must destroy the false image of the terrorists as religious freedom fighters. We must discredit their financial supporters
as charities. We must expose the corrupt countries or organizations
that give terrorists free passage, access to resources, or training camps.
All are legitimate targets in our media war against the terrorists.

To support America's message, America must continually gather
evidence against terror and feed damaging material to the media.

To use the media, our leaders must understand the news cycle.
Our people must have the time to find solid, interesting stories.

We must release our media attacks correctly. We should provide
stories to the media when news is slow and they can get attention.

We should time the stories to arouse the press's curiosity.
Reporters should have easy access to people and evidence.

The best time to release a hot story is right before the nightly news.
To build a more complex story, we can use the daylong news cycle.

Everyone attacks with fire. 2
You must create five different situations with fire and be able
to adjust to them.

3You start a fire inside the enemy's camp.
Then attack the enemy's periphery.

5You launch a fire attack, but the enemy remains calm.
Wait and do not attack.

7The fire reaches its height.
Follow its path if you can.
If you can't follow it, stay where you are.

10Spreading fires on the outside of camp can kill.
You can't always get fire inside the enemy's camp.
Take your time in spreading it.

13Set the fire when the wind is at your back.
Don't attack into the wind.
Daytime winds last a long time.
Night winds fade quickly.

17Every army must know how to adjust to the five possible
attacks by fire.
Use many men to guard against them.

2. We must learn how to get our message out through the media because our actions are attacked in the media. There are different tactics we must learn to use and defend ourselves against.

First, we must expose the duplicity of counties that support terrorists. If we are successful, we can threaten their interests.

If the targeted nations successfully maintain an innocent image, we must hold off on any attack until we can undermine that image.

When news hostile to terrorist supporters reaches its peak, we should target the specific people or places in those stories militarily. If we cannot act on the specifics in the story, we should not act.

Sometimes, we cannot get information on the terror-supporting nations directly. However, we can investigate outside organizations that secretly support terror and build those stories over time.

We should leverage our stories in the media by using the hot issues of the day. We should not compete with a hot news story. Some topics, especially those in newspapers or on talk radio, can last for quite some time, while those on the nightly news tend to fade quickly.

We must constantly evaluate the news to identify the opportunities to target terrorists. We need to have people in this war focused on developing stories and protecting us against lies.

When you use fire to assist your attacks, you are clever. 3
Water can add force to an attack.
You can also use water to disrupt an enemy's forces.
It does not, however, take his resources.

You win in battle by getting the opportunity to attack. 4
It is dangerous if you fail to study how to accomplish this
achievement.
As commander, you cannot waste your opportunities.

4We say:
A wise leader plans success.
A good general studies it.
If there is little to be gained, don't act.
If there is little to win, do not use your men.
If there is no danger, don't fight.

10As the leader, you cannot let your anger interfere with the
success of your forces.
As commander, you cannot let yourself become enraged
before you go to battle.
Join the battle only when it is in your advantage to act.
If there is no advantage in joining a battle, stay put.

14Anger can change back into happiness.
Rage can change back into joy.
A nation once destroyed cannot be brought back to life.
Dead men do not return to the living.

3   We are wise to use media attacks to put heat on terrorists. Using the force of change (water) such as technological innovation puts pressure on terrorists, and it can destroy their plans, but change doesn't undermine their infrastructure like using the media does.

4   We must constantly be searching in every story for the specifics that vilify terrorists' actions. We are at a disadvantage as long as we lack the skills to clearly communicate this message. This has been one of the greatest weaknesses in our War on Terror thus far.

We must realize that many people in the world want to think the worst of America and its leaders. We must take this fact into account in our communication plans. We must make sure that the information we offer cannot be used against us. If the story doesn't clearly expose the evil of the terrorists, we shouldn't use it. If a story doesn't clearly expose their duplicity, we need not promote it.

As leaders in the War on Terror, Americans cannot afford to get angry at the media. That doesn't help us fight this kind of war. Our spokespeople can never let themselves get visibly upset when facing the press. Before we address the media, we must make sure that the information we provide makes the evil of terrorism clear. If the information doesn't portray terrorists as evil, we need not offer it.

Our unhappiness with the media can be changed into happiness. The hostility of the media can be turned into respect. If we lose this war, our civilization cannot be rescued. If we do not change the media story, many innocent people will die.

[18]This fact must make a wise leader cautious.
A good general is on guard.

[20]Your philosophy must be to keep the nation peaceful and
the army intact.

♦ ♦ ♦

We cannot be too sensitive in dealing with the media. We must always be in a position to defend against their attacks.

If we win the battle in the media, the world can be safe from terrorists and our soldiers do not have to die.

✦ ✦ ✦

Chapter 13

用間

Using Spies: Acquiring Intelligence

Sun Tzu saves his most important topic for last. If the 9/11 Commission taught us anything, it was that America's intelligence-gathering abilities are deeply flawed. Many of our weaknesses in gathering information have been self-inflicted. After Vietnam, many politicians worked actively against funding intelligence gathering. Others thought that technology was the key to intelligence. We neglected what Sun Tzu identified as the only important source of information: people, what we now call human intelligence (or HUMINT, in government-speak), as if there was any other kind.

On the battlefield, the US has the best real-time information systems in the world. However, the real purpose of good intelligence is to avoid the types of battles we fought in Iraq and Afghanistan. Good information allows us to attack the terrorists and their organizations directly, making them targets that are as visible as the states that support terrorism.

According to classical strategy, spies must be used in the War on Terror, both to discover information and to send the terrorists false information. Today, much is made of gathering information, but Sun Tzu considered communicating false information at least as important. Knowledge is the basis of all strategy. If we can set the terrorists up to act on bad information, they can be more easily killed or captured.

Of all the chapters in *The Art of War*, this one is the easiest to directly adapt to the central issues of the War on Terror.

Using Spies

All successful armies require thousands of men. 1
They invade and march thousands of miles.
Whole families are destroyed.
Other families must be heavily taxed.
Every day, a large amount of money must be spent.

[6]Internal and external events force people to move.
They are unable to work while on the road.
They are unable to find and hold a useful job.
This affects 70 percent of thousands of families.

[10]You can watch and guard for years.
Then a single battle can determine victory in a day.
Despite this, bureaucrats worship the value of their salary
money too dearly.
They remain ignorant of the enemy's condition.
The result is cruel.

[15]They are not leaders of men.
They are not servants of the state.
They are not masters of victory.

Acquiring Intelligence

1 The War on Terror requires hundreds of thousands of troops. We have had to move our forces halfway around the world. War is terribly costly, both because it inevitably costs lives and because prosecuting it on a day-to-day basis costs the taxpayers money. The longer this war continues, the more it will cost.

The cost of conducting the War on Terror also includes its negative impact on the economy, not only here but in the Middle East. It took America literally years to recover from 9/11. Everyone, even those who aren't directly fighting, pays the price of being at war.

We have been under attack by Islamic terrorists for years. They hope that a truly horrific attack with weapons of mass destruction will give them a real victory. Despite this threat, for most of this time our government has been more concerned about its budgets than fighting terrorists. The result of slashing our budgets for gathering intelligence has been devastating.

The politicians who undermined our ability to gather intelligence were not acting in our best interests. They were not helping America or our cause. They put us at a disadvantage in this war.

[18]You need a creative leader and a worthy commander.
You must move your troops to the right places to beat others.
You must accomplish your attack and escape unharmed.
This requires foreknowledge.
You can obtain foreknowledge.
You can't get it from demons or spirits.
You can't see it from professional experience.
You can't check it with analysis.
You can only get it from other people.
You must always know the enemy's situation.

You must use five types of spies. 2
You need local spies.
You need inside spies.
You need double agents.
You need doomed spies.
You need surviving spies.

[7]You need all five types of spies.
No one must discover your methods.
You will then be able to put together a true picture.
This is the commander's most valuable resource.

[11]You need local spies.
Get them by hiring people from the countryside.

[13]You need inside spies.
Win them by subverting government officials.

We must choose leaders who are creative and trustworthy. We have to move our troops to where the terrorists are a gathering threat. We must be able to attack them without losing our own people. All of this requires knowledge about their plans.

We can get information about their plans, but it doesn't come from thin air or magic. None of our professionals can tell us what the terrorists will do next out of their experience alone. Analyzing raw information before the action doesn't give us this knowledge. We need to have people inside these organizations who know their plans and who can tell us what the terrorists are doing.

2 We should think of spies not as James Bonds but as communication channels, go-betweens, and conduits of information. Developing and maintaining a network of information channels is the key to intelligence. Five types of spies give us insight into the five key factors that define the terrorists' position: their philosophy, the climate, the ground, their leaders, and their methods.

All five types of information sources are necessary to put together a complete picture of what the terrorists are planning. For this to work, we must keep our information sources a secret. The channels of information we develop are our most valuable resource.

Local spies provide information outer layer of support organizations that work with terrorist within a given area.

Inside spies are operatives who work as part of the infrastructure of terrorist networks.

¹⁵You need double agents.
Discover enemy agents and convert them.

¹⁷You need doomed spies.
Deceive professionals into being captured.
Let them know your orders.
They then take those orders to your enemy.

²¹You need surviving spies.
Someone must return with a report.

Your job is to build a complete army. 3
No relations are as intimate as the ones with spies.
No rewards are too generous for spies.
No work is as secret as that of spies.

⁵If you aren't clever and wise, you can't use spies.
If you aren't fair and just, you can't use spies.
If you can't see the small subtleties, you won't get the truth
from spies.

⁸Pay attention to small, trifling details!
Spies are helpful in every area.

¹⁰Spies are the first to hear information, so they must not
spread information.
Spies who give your location or talk to others must be killed
along with those to whom they have talked.

Double agents are spies who have been working for terrorists but who we are able to win over to our cause.

Doomed spies are mercenaries who think they know our plans. We should put these mercenaries in positions where they might be captured by terrorists. We can then use them to communicate information to set the terrorists up to be killed or captured.

Surviving spies are those who can return from within a terrorist organization, reporting on what the terrorists are planning.

3 America cannot have a complete defense without a network of spies. This is the most delicate part of building our forces. No matter how much we spend on information, it is well worth the price. We must keep this information out of the press and public.

In the past, we have undermined our information channels. We have unjustly abused those, such as Ahmed Chalabi, a former opponent of Saddam's. No information source is perfect, but unless we factor in the self-interest of spies, we cannot get to the truth.

In the end, it is often the small details that are telling. This is why we must collect as many details about the terrorists as we can.

The secret to successfully gathering information on the terrorists is getting that information quickly before it is generally known. Spying has always been a dangerous business because critical information is always a matter of life and death.

You may want to attack an army's position. 4
You may want to attack a certain fortification.
You may want to kill people in a certain place.
You must first know the guarding general.
You must know his left and right flanks.
You must know his hierarchy.
You must know the way in.
You must know where different people are stationed.
You must demand this information from your spies.

10You want to know the enemy spies in order to convert
them into your men.
You must find sources of information and bribe them.
You must bring them in with you.
You must obtain them as double agents and use them as
your emissaries.

14Do this correctly and carefully.
You can contact both local and inside spies and obtain their
support.
Do this correctly and carefully.
You create doomed spies by deceiving professionals.
You can use them to give false information.
Do this correctly and carefully.
You must have surviving spies capable of bringing you infor-
mation at the right time.

4 In the War on Terror, we must find out where the terrorists are hiding. We must know where they hide their weapons. We must find their leaders at a certain time and place.

To do this successfully, we must know the decision-makers within terrorist organizations. We must know the people they trust. We must know their chain of command. We must know how to find where they meet. We must know where their people are stationed. This is the information that we should focus on in building our information network around the terrorist organizations.

Terrorists almost certainly have people spying on us. Instead of putting them on trial, we should be working to convert them to our cause. The information they have is invaluable, and most of them can be bribed. They will join us if we give them the proper incentives. Once we start winning over these double agents, we can use them to recruit other people within their organizations.

Infiltrating terrorist organizations is a delicate matter, but it can be done over time. We can develop source who know terrorist areas and terrorist leaders. To contact them, we need a network of people who can work easily within the Muslim world. Some of our operatives will be captured, but they can be used to give misleading information that will confuse and disorganize the terrorists. We have to plan this carefully ahead of time. We can also bring our people who have been working within terrorist organizations back when they discover information that is immediately important.

²¹These are the five different types of intelligence work.
You must be certain to master them all.
You must be certain to create double agents.
You cannot afford to be too cost conscious in creating these double agents.

This technique created the success of ancient Shang. 5
This is how the Shang held their dynasty.

³You must always be careful of your success.
Learn from Lu Ya of Shang.

⁵Be a smart commander and a good general.
You do this by using your best and brightest people for spying.
This is how you achieve the greatest success.
This is how you meet the necessities of war.
The whole army's position and ability to move depends on these spies.

✦ ✦ ✦

✦ ✦ ✦

In the War on Terror, our most valuable tool is this complete information network. In Sun Tzu's view, it is worth any price because good information can eliminate many of the other costs and much of the waste of war. The foundation of this network is the agents that we convert from working for the terrorists.

5 In the end, all wars are won by those with the best information. The War on Terror is the most information-intensive war in history.

Because it is a media war, we can win it only if we get better at gathering and communicating information on the terrorists.

We must pick good leaders who are willing to appoint the best heads for our intelligence agencies. We must make spying respectable again so that it attracts the best possible people. In the end, this is how we will win this war and minimize its costs. Everything that we do with our army in the Middle East and our security forces at home depends on the quality of our information.

♦ ♦ ♦

♦ ♦ ♦

Summary

The Ten Keys to Winning

Classical strategy provides a framework for understanding any competitive situation. Because most people—especially those in the media—lack such a framework, they have failed to properly analyze the strategic progress of this war. Only once we learn to see the war as a battle of positioning are we on the road to understanding which moves are important and which are not.

The attack on the World Trade Center was important for terrorists because it positioned them as a force to be reckoned with. Though Islamic terrorists have operated for centuries throughout the Muslim world, this attack made it clear that the threat they represent has worldwide significance. By refocusing their efforts on the West, the terrorists discovered that every successful attack increased their visibility in the media and their popularity among the Muslim populace.

The first key to success is moving the battlefield back into the Muslim world. Strategy means picking the right battleground. After overthrowing the radical Islamic government in Afghanistan and the national socialist government in Iraq, America forced the terrorists to fight within Islamic countries. Increased terrorist strikes in the Muslim community decrease terrorists' support among fellow Muslims. After terror strikes increased within Saudi

Arabia, support for bin Laden was reduced from 96 percent of the population to less than 25 percent. By moving the war to Islamic countries, we are putting the terrorists on scattering ground, which destroys Muslim unity.

Strategy also teaches that we must learn from successful wars. In recent history, Algeria and Peru have been two of the nations hardest hit by terrorism within their own borders. In Algeria, terrorists launched up to thirty simultaneous attacks in 1995, killing hundreds of people in a day. In Peru, the Shining Path killed over thirty thousand people in the same decade. However, by 1999, both nations had largely defeated terrorism. The next nine keys to strategy are drawn both from Sun Tzu and the experience of these two countries.

The second key to success is treating terrorists as criminals rather than rebels. At first, both Alain Garcia in Peru and Muhammad Boudiaf in Algeria tried to understand and address the "root causes" of terrorism, only to see terrorist activity grow dramatically more widespread and violent. After Garcia lost reelection to Fujimori and Boudiaf was assassinated, these countries' new leaders began treating terrorists like criminals, focusing on killing them before they could kill others. As strategy teaches, choosing the right philosophy is all important. After this, terrorism began to decline.

The third key is that the leaders of the Muslim world must be united against terror. Strategy teaches that unity is strength. In both Algeria and Peru, the political, business, and religious leaders finally joined together in their determination not to surrender to the fear and uncertainty that is the chief weapon of the terrorists. It doesn't matter if Muslim leaders unite out of trust, greed, or fear of the United States as long as they join together.

The fourth key is that we must make assassination more difficult. Strategy teaches that an army can be overturned by killing its commander. Assassination, invented in 1092 by al-Hasan ibn-al-

Sabbah and his Ashishin, is the oldest form of terror. Leaders in Algeria and Peru initially tried to protect themselves by concentrating and fortifying their key people in well-defended compounds, but that approach created an easy target for terrorists. Later, both countries dispersed their key people, making it harder to organize surveillance and assassinations. Already Muslim leaders in Pakistan, Saudi Arabia, Iraq, and Jordan have faced assassination attempts and should respond in the same way.

The fifth key is creating barriers, not to stop terror but to slow it down. Strategy teaches that obstacles are one of the three dimensions that characterize the ground. Terrorists need quick, spectacular strikes meaning they need unobstructed ground. Since their forces are small, they can move faster than defense forces. Defense forces cannot stop terrorists, but they can create obstacles to slow them down. By making terror a long marathon rather than a fast sprint, defensive forces can leverage the strength of their size.

The sixth key is luring terrorists into fixed positions. In a long war, terrorists need hospitals, weapons depots, training camps, and other fixed sites. Both Algeria and Peru played to this need, creating seeming "safe havens" for terrorists. For example, Algerian forces stayed out of the Mitidja plain and the town of Blida. Once the terrorists were convinced that these areas were safe, they built up their resources in them, allowing authorities to attack at a time of their choosing. American and Iraqi forces used the same technique to lure terrorists into Falluja in Iraq.

The seventh key is winning both the physical war and the media war. Suppressing the news leaves the population open to terrorist propaganda. Both Algeria and Peru learned to encourage professional journalists who reported the truth about terrorism. The more journalists learned about the terrorists and their victims, the less sympathetic the media became. This process may have already begun in the Middle East as well. The videos of beheading may give the terrorists the publicity they seek, but these videos make it more difficult for the world media to portray terrorists as some form of freedom fighters.

The eighth key is penetrating the outer shells of the terrorist network. Defense forces in Peru and Algeria infiltrated the groups that provided money, information, surveillance, and logistical support to the terrorists. Working from within, they fed the terrorists misinformation and were eventually able to identify and target the core groups. This is why the War on Terror can only be won by Muslims. Only Muslims can infiltrate and disrupt the support systems that make terrorism possible.

The ninth key is challenging the economics of terror. As Sun Tzu teaches, all wars are economic. Terrorist organizations cannot survive by fund-raising alone, especially as their popularity wanes and their outer shells are compromised. They need drug money, smuggling, funding from supporting states, extortion, racketeering, and bank robberies to survive. Cutting off these illegal sources of funds is critical. Exposing these crimes also further changes the perception of the terrorists among the Muslim people. The more criminal activities the terrorists are involved in, the weaker their claim to religious superiority and divine justification.

The tenth key is economic freedom. In Algeria and Peru, instead of letting the fight against terror consume all their resources or make their regimes more economically oppressive, both nations reformed their economies. This strengthened economic activity which in turn strengthened support for the state. Lack of economic freedom is the true root cause of terrorism. The greatest accomplishment of the War on Terror will be to force the governments of the Islamic world to liberalize their economic policies. Secular democracy may or may not be compatible with Islam in its present form, but Malaysia has already proven that the Muslim world is ready for economic opportunity.

✦ ✦ ✦

Index of Topics in *The Art of War*

This index identifies significant topics, keyed to the chapters, block numbers (big numbers in text), and line numbers (tiny numbers). The format is chapter:block.lines.

About the Translator and Author

Gary Gagliardi is recognized as America's leading expert on Sun Tzu's *The Art of War*. An award-winning author and businessperson, he is known for his ability to put sophisticated concepts into simple, easy-to-understand terms. He appears on hundreds of talk shows nationwide, providing strategic insight on the breaking news.

Gary began studying the Chinese classic more than thirty years ago, applying its principles first to his own career, then to building a successful business, and finally in training the world's largest organizations to be more competitive. He has spoken all over the world on a variety of topics concerning competition, from modern technology to ancient history. His books have been translated into many languages, including Japanese, Korean, Russian, and Spanish.

Gary began using Sun Tzu's competitive principles in a successful corporate career but soon started his own software company. In 1990, he wrote his first *Art of War* adaptation for his company's salespeople. By 1992, his company was one of *Inc.* magazine's 500 fastest-growing privately held companies in America. After he won the U.S. Chamber of Commerce **Blue Chip Quality Award** and became an Ernst and Young **Entrepreneur of the Year** finalist, his customers—AT&T, GE, and Motorola, among others—began inviting him to speak at their conferences. Jardin's, the original Hong Kong trading company known as "The Noble House," became one of his partners and even gave him the honor of firing the noontime cannon in Hong Kong's harbor. After becoming a multimillionaire when he sold his software company in 1997, he continued teaching *The Art of War* around the world.

Gary has authored several breakthrough works on *The Art of War*. In 1999, he translated each Chinese character to demonstrate its equation-like symmetry. In 2003, his work *The Art of War Plus The Ancient Chinese Revealed* won the **Independent Publishers Book Award** as the year's best new multicultural nonfiction work. In 2004, his adaptation of Sun Tzu's principles to marketing, *The Art of War Plus The Art of Marketing*, was selected as one of the three best business books by the **Ben Franklin Book Awards committee**. In 2004, he released a new work that explains the many hidden aspects of Sun Tzu's text, *The Art of War Plus Its Amazing Secrets*, which was selected as a **Highlighted Title** by Independent Publishers.

Gary has also written a large number of other adaptations of *The Art of War*, applying Sun Tzu's methods to areas such as career building, management, marketing, selling, small business, and even romance and parenting.

Gary lives near Seattle with his wife.

Art of War Gift Books

The Mastering Strategy Series

Sun Tzu's The Art of War Plus The Ancient Chinese Revealed
See the original! Each original Chinese character individually translated.

Sun Tzu's The Art of War Plus Its Amazing Secrets
Learn the hidden secrets! The deeper meaning of *bing-fa* explained.

The Warrior Class: 306 Lessons in Strategy
The complete study guide! The most extensive analysis of *The Art of War* ever written.

Career and Business Series

Sun Tzu's The Art of War Plus The Art of Career Building
For everyone! Use Sun Tzu's lessons to advance your career.

Sun Tzu's The Art of War Plus The Art of Sales
For salespeople! Use Sun Tzu's lessons to win sales and keep customers.

Sun Tzu's The Art of War Plus The Art of Management
For managers! Use Sun Tzu's lessons one managing teams more effectively.

Sun Tzu's The Art of War Plus Strategy for Sales Managers
For managers! Use Sun Tzu's lessons to direct salespeople more effectively.

Sun Tzu's The Art of War Plus The Art of Small Business
For business owners! Use Sun Tzu's lessons in building your own business.

Sun Tzu's The Art of War Plus The Art of Marketing
For marketing professionals! Use Sun Tzu's lessons to win marketing warfare.

Life Strategies Series

Sun Tzu's The Art of War Plus The Warrior's Apprentice
A first book of strategy for young adults.

Sun Tzu's The Art of War Plus The Art of Love
For lifelong love! *Bing-fa* applied to finding, winning, and keeping love alive.

Sun Tzu's The Art of War Plus The Art of Parenting Teens
For every parent! Strategy applied to protecting, guiding, and motivating teens.

Current Events Series

Sun Tzu's The Art of War Plus Strategy against Terror
An examination of the War on Terror using Sun Tzu's timeless principles.

Audio and Video

Amazing Secrets of The Art of War: Audio with book
1 1/2 Hours 2 CD set

Amazing Secrets of *The Art of War*: Video with book
1 1/2 Hours VHS

To Order On-line: Visit www.BooksOnStrategy.com
Fax Orders: 206-546-9756. Voice: 206-533-9357.

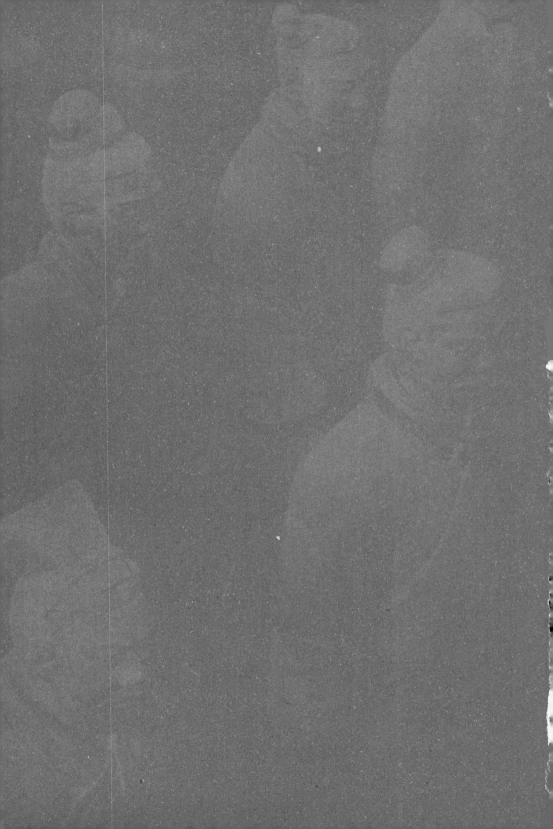